How to AVOID

the PAIN and

SUFFERING of

PROBATE!!

by
Rolland G. (Rollie) Riesberg

Rolland G. (Rollie) Riesberg
LCR Estate Planning Services, LLC, Book Division
Morrow, GA

ISBN: 978-0-9907244-9-0
Library of Congress Control Number: 2016944306

10 9 8 7 6 5 4 3 2   061016

This book may be ordered through booksellers or by contacting the Printer.

♾ This paper meets the requirements of ANSI/NISO Z39.48-1992 (Permanence of Paper)

TABLE OF CONTENTS

HOW TO AVOID THE PAIN AND SUFFERING OF PROBATE

(THE Living Trust Book)

By Rolland G. (Rollie) Riesberg

INTRODUCTION

This is the MUST READ 'Go To' Book for what to do:
1) Before the death of a dear loved one.
2) After the death of a dear loved one.

URGENT NOTICE: If you are going to die someday, you **MUST READ** this Book---before you do!

We know that you love your dear loved ones and immediate family members and you don't want them to experience the pain and suffering and hardship of extensive time delays and exorbitant loss of family assets (money, housing/land, investments/savings, use of your personal belongings) and immediate access to your checking account money from having to go through the Probate process of settling the estate upon your death. And in most cases, all assets are "frozen" (non-accessible to remaining family members) until the court-directed Probate process is completed---which could take years. Your spouse having their **deeply broken heart** from the loss of you is just too much for them to endure, while contending with the traumatic probability of temporarily or permanently losing access to the family home and money for food, utilities and other urgently needed living expenses.

We are writing this book because we love and care about you, the readers of our Book. We ourselves, our family members, and many of our good friends and business associates have had to endure the pain and suffering of Probate in our lives. Once you have read this Book, you will then have acquired the knowledge to help you and your family make the needed decisions to help you **"Avoid the Pain and Suffering of Probate."**

As the Author of this extremely IMPORTANT Book, it is not my intention to be critical but to be helpful.

(Mom & Dad)
Mae & Ralph Riesberg
Wedding Photo (1933)

Loretta and Rollie's Wedding 1964

(Loretta's Mom & Dad)
Douglas & Marietta Robertson
Just Married 1936

Rollie 1961

Rollie in Hawaii with his Dad,
Summer 1953

Loretta Robertson 1961
Delta Air Lines Stewardess

CHAPTER ONE

THE IMPORTANCE OF PROPER ESTATE PLANNING

What is Estate Planning?

Estate Planning is the process of anticipating and arranging for the distribution of your estate during your lifetime, i.e. creating a definite plan for managing your wealth and material assets while you are alive and distributing them to your loved ones and heirs after your death.

What Does an Estate Consist of?

(1) Real Estate (your residence and rental property).
(2) Business Interests/Ownership (sole proprietorships, partnerships, corporations, joint-ownership properties).
(3) Investments (stocks, bonds, mutual funds, annuities, tax sheltered accounts).
(4) Retirement Plans (401(k), 403(b), 457, Traditional, Roth & SIMPLE IRAs, SEP).
(5) Life Insurance Policies.
(6) Personal Effects (personal belongings, including heirlooms, antiques, jewelry and collectibles).

Why Do You Need Estate Planning?

You need to do the proper Estate Planning to help you and your immediate family avoid the obstacles that adversely affect the preservation of the wealth you have accumulated during your life time. These obstacles are:

(1) Probate process
(2) Federal and State Estate Taxes (Death Tax)
(3) Conservatorship (The Probate Court/court appointee making those "health care issues" decisions for you instead of you and your spouse making those critical decisions for you.) For instance, when your health condition deteriorates to a certain point, will you receive your needed health care at home, or in an assisted living facility, a nursing home or a hospice facility?

CHAPTER TWO

WHAT IS PROBATE?

The History and Summary of Probate

Countries whose legal systems evolved from the British common law system, such as the United States, typically use the **Probate** system for distributing property at death. **Probate** is a process where 1) the decedent's purported **Will**, if any, is entered in court, 2) after hearing evidence from the representative of the estate, the court decides if the **Will** is valid, 3) a personal representative is appointed by the court as a fiduciary to close out the estate, 4) known and unknown creditors are notified (through direct notice or publication in the media), 5) claims are paid out (if funds remain) in order of priority governed by state statute, 6) remaining funds are distributed to beneficiaries named in the **Will**, or heirs if there is no **Will**, and 7) the **Probate** judge closes out the estate (all claims against the estate have been settled).

In summary, if there is a **Will** or a **Will** does not exist, upon the death of each spouse, usually the estate will be subject to some form of Probate. Probate is the mandatory court proceeding which completes all the legal and financial matters of the decedent.

After all assets have been inventoried and all creditor claims have been paid, the **Probate** court changes the titling of all the assets from the name of the decedent to the name/s of the beneficiary/s named in the **Will**. This procedure usually takes from one to three years, and often longer.

CHAPTER THREE

THE PROS AND CONS OF PROBATE

The Advantages of Probate

If the decedent (deceased) did not even leave behind a piece of paper giving instructions on how he/she wanted the estate to be settled, then the **Probate** process has some helpful advantages, which are:

(1) Providing a forum for resolving disputes (estate settlement contests).
(2) Establishes an executor for the estate and supervises the work of the executor.
(3) Inventories and appraises all assets and debts of the decedent.
(4) Provides for the payment of creditor claims against the estate.
(5) Once resolution of the estate is established, re-titling of assets and distribution to candidate beneficiaries will be accomplished in accordance with state and federal **Probate** laws.

The Disadvantages of Probate

Please NOTE: These Disadvantages pertain to a situation where the decedent created a valid **Will** before passing. For the benefits of court supervision in **Probate**, your family will more than likely pay an exorbitant price for going through the **Probate** process.

(1) Excessive Fees: Attorney's, Executor's, Appraisal; and court filing fees and bond premiums can be exorbitant.
(2) Excessive Delays: The **Probate** process takes between six months and three years, on average, depending on the complexity of the estate.
(3) Time-frame for Estate Taxes to be Paid: Within nine months of the death of the decedent.
(4) Family Private Information Becoming
   Public Record: **Probate** records in most states will reveal every detail of the deceased family's financial life, as made available by the County Courthouse. These records, which include heir names, addresses, phone numbers and dollar amounts to be received, are available for public review and scrutiny.
(5) Property Owned in Other States: The **Probate** process must take place in each state where the decedent owned real estate and other assets.
(6) The Psychological Impact: Rigid, inflexible **Probate** court proceedings are a constant reminder of the death of the dear family member. More often than not, heirs feel trapped, helpless, controlled and frustrated by court actions.

CHAPTER FOUR

WHAT ARE WILLS?

A **Will** is a document in which a person specifies the method to be applied in the management and distribution of a person's estate after his or her death.

A **Will** is the legal instrument that permits a person, the testator, to make decisions on how his or her estate will be managed and distributed after his or her death. At Common Law, an instrument disposing of Personal Property was called a "testament," whereas a **Will** disposed of real property. Over time the distinction has disappeared so that a **Will** sometimes called a "last will and testament," disposes of both real and personal property.

If a person does not leave a **Will**, or the **Will** is declared invalid, the person will have died intestate, resulting in the distribution of the estate according to the laws of Descent and Distribution of the state in which the person resided. Because of the importance of a **Will**, the law requires it to have certain elements to be valid. Apart from these elements, a **Will** may be ruled invalid if the testator made the **Will** as the result of UNDUE INFLUENCE, FRAUD, or mistake.

A **Will** serves a variety of important purposes. It enables a person to select his or her heirs rather than allowing the state laws of Descent and Distribution to choose the heirs, who although blood relatives, might be people the testator dislikes or with whom he/she is unacquainted. A **Will** allows a person to decide which individual could best serve as the executor of his/her estate, distributing the property fairly to the beneficiaries while protecting their interests, rather than allowing a court to appoint a stranger to serve as administrator. A **Will** safeguards a person's right to select an individual to serve as guardian to raise his/her young children in the event of his/her death.

1. Requirements of a Will

A valid **Will** cannot exist unless three essential elements are present. First, there must be a competent testator. Second, the document purporting to be a **Will** must meet the execution requirements of statutes, often called the Statute of Wills, designed to ensure that the document is not a fraud but is the honest expression of the testator's intention. Third, it must be clear that the testator intended the document to have the legal effect of a **Will**.

If a **Will** does not satisfy these requirements, any person who would have a financial interest in the estate under the laws of Descent and Distribution can start an action in the **Probate** court to challenge the validity of the **Will**. The persons who inherit under the **Will** are proponents of the **Will** and defend it against such an attack. This proceeding is known as a **Will** contest. If the people who oppose the admission of the **Will** to **Probate** are successful, the testator's estate will be distributed according to the laws of Descent and Distribution or the provisions of an earlier **Will**, depending on the facts of the case.

Competent Testator:

A competent testator is a person who is of sound mind and requisite age at the time that he/she makes the **Will**, not at the date of his/her death when it takes effect. Anyone over a minimum age, usually eighteen, is legally capable of making a **Will** as long as he/she is competent. A person under the minimum age dies intestate (regardless of efforts to make a **Will**), and his/her property will be distributed according to the laws of Descent and Distribution.

An individual has testamentary capacity (sound mind) if he/she is able to understand the nature and extent of his/her property, the natural objects of his/her bounty (to whom he/she would like to leave the estate), and the nature of the testamentary act (the distribution of his/her property when he/she dies). He/she must also understand how these elements are related so that he/she can express the method of disposition of property.

A testator is considered mentally incompetent (incapable of making a **Will**) if he/she has a recognized type of mental deficiency, such as a severe mental illness. Mere eccentricities, such as the refusal to bathe, are not considered insane delusions, nor are mistaken beliefs or prejudices about family members. A person who uses drugs or alcohol can validly execute a **Will** as long as he/she is not under the influence of drugs or intoxicated at the time he/she makes the Will. Illiteracy, old age, or severe physical illness do not automatically deprive a person of a testamentary capacity, but they are factors to be considered along with the particular facts of the case.

2. Execution Requirements for Wills

Every state has **statutes** prescribing the formalities to be observed in making a valid **Will**. The requirements relate to the writing, signing, witnessing, or attestation of the **Will** in addition to its publication. These legislative safeguards prevent tentative, doubt-ful, or coerced expressions of desire from controlling the manner in which a person's estate is distributed.

Writing: Wills usually must be in writing but can be in any language and inscribed with any material or device on any substance that results in a permanent record. Generally, most **Wills** are printed on paper to satisfy this requirement. Many states do not recognize as valid a **Will** that is handwritten and signed by the testator. In states that do accept such a **Will**, called a holographic **Will**, it usually must observe the formalities of execution unless exempted by statute. Some jurisdictions also require that such **Wills** be dated by the testator's hand.

Signature: A **Will** must be signed by the testator. Any mark, such as an X, a zero, a check mark, or a name intended by a competent testator to be his/her signature to authenticate the **Will**, is a valid signing. Some states permit another person to sign a **Will** for a testator at the testator's direction or request or with his/her consent. Many state statutes require that the testator's signature be at the end of the **Will**. If it is not, the entire **Will** may be invalidated in those states, and the testator's property will pass according to the laws of Descent and Distribution. The testator should sign the **Will** before the witnesses sign, but the reverse order is usually permissible if all sign as part of a single transaction.

Witnesses: Statutes require a certain number of witnesses to a **Will**. Most require two although others mandate three. The witnesses sign the **Will** and must be able to attest (certify) that the testator was competent at the time he/she made the **Will**. Though there are no formal qualifications for a witness. It is important that a witness not have financial interest in the **Will**. If a witness has an interest, his/her testimony about the circumstances will be suspect because he/she will profit by its admission to **Probate**. In most states such witnesses must either "purge" their interest under the **Will** (forfeit their rights under the **Will**) or be barred from testifying, thereby defeating the testator's testamentary plan. If, however, the witness also would inherit under the laws of Descent and Distribution should the **Will** be invalidated, he/she will forfeit only the interest in excess of the amount he/she would receive if the **Will** were voided.

   Acknowledgement: A testator is usually required to publish the **Will**---that is, to declare to the witnesses that the instrument is his/her **Will**. This declaration is called an Acknowledgement. No state requires, however, that the witnesses know the contents of the **Will**.

   Although some states require a testator to sign the **Will** in the presence of witnesses, the majority require only an acknowledgement of the signature. If a testator shows the signature on a **Will** that he/she has already signed to a witness and acknowledges that it is his/her signature, the **Will** is thereby acknowledged.

   Attestation: An attestation clause is a certificate signed by the witnesses to a **Will** reciting performance of the formalities of execution that the witnesses observed. It usually is not required for a **Will** to be valid, but in some states it is evidence that the statements made in the attestation are true.

3. **Testator's Intent**

   For a **Will** to be admitted to **Probate**, it must be clear that the testator acted freely in expressing his/her testamentary intention. A **Will** executed as a result of undue influence, fraud, or mistake can be declared completely or partially void in a **Probate** proceeding.

   Undue Influence: Undue influence is pressure that takes away a person's free will to make decisions, substituting the will of the influencer. A court will find undue influence if the testator was capable of being influenced, improper influence was was exerted on the testator, and the testamentary provisions reflect the effect of such influence. Mere advice, persuasion, affection, or kindness does not alone constitute undue influence.

   Questions of undue influence typically arise when a **Will** deals unjustly with persons believed to be the natural objects of the testator's bounty. However, undue influence is not established by inequality of the provisions of the **Will**, because this would interfere with the testator's ability to dispose of the property as he/she pleases. Examples of undue influence include threats of violence or criminal prosecution of the testator, or the threat to abandon a sick testator.

Fraud: Fraud differs from undue influence in that the former involves **Misrepresentation** of essential facts to another to persuade him/her to make and sign a **Will** that will benefit the person who misrepresents the facts. The testator still acts freely in making and signing the **Will**.

The two types of fraud are fraud in the execution and fraud in the inducement. When a person is deceived by another as to the character or contents of the document he/she is signing, he/she is the victim of fraud in the execution. Fraud in the execution includes a situation where the contents of the **Will** are knowingly misrepresented to the testator by someone who will benefit from the misrepresentation.

Fraud in the inducement occurs when a person knowingly makes a **Will** but its terms are based on material misrepresentations of facts made to the testator by someone who will ultimately benefit.

Persons deprived of benefiting under a **Will** because of fraud or undue influence can obtain relief only by contesting the **Will**. If a court finds fraud or undue influence, it may prevent the wrongdoer from receiving any benefit from the **Will** and may distribute the property to those who contested the **Will**.

Mistake: When a testator intended to execute his/her **Will** but by mistake signed the wrong document, that document will not be enforced. Such mistakes often occur when a **Husband and Wife** draft mutual **Wills**. The document that bears the testator's signature does not represent his/her testamentary intent, and therefore his/her property cannot be distributed according to its terms.

4. Special Types of Wills

Some states have statutes that recognize certain kinds of **Wills** that are executed with less formality than ordinary **Wills**, but only when the **Wills** are made under circumstances that reduce the possibility of fraud.

Holographic Wills: A holographic **Will** is completely written and signed in the handwriting of the testator, such as a letter that specifically discusses his/her intended distribution of the estate after his/her death. Many states do not recognize the validity of holographic **Wills**, and those that do require that the formalities of execution be followed.

Nuncupative Wills: A nuncupative **Will** is an oral **Will**. Most states do not recognize the validity of such **Wills** because of the greater likelihood of fraud, but those that do impose certain requirements. The **Will** must be made during the testator's last sickness or in expectation of imminent death. The testator must indicate to the witnesses that he/she wants them to witness his/her oral **Will**. Such a **Will** can dispose of only personal, not real, property.

Soldiers' and Sailors' Wills: Several states have laws that relax the execution requirements for **Wills** made by soldiers and sailors while on active military duty or at sea. In these situations a testator's oral or handwritten **Will** is capable of passing personal property. Where such **Wills** are recognized, statutes often stipulate that they are valid for only a certain period of time after the testator has left the service. In other instances, however, the **Will** remains valid.

5. Revocation of a Will

A **Will** is ambulatory, which means that a competent testator may change or revoke it at any time before his/her death. Revocation of a **Will** occurs when a person who has made a **Will** takes some action to indicate that he/she no longer wants its provisions to be binding and the law abides by his/her decision.

For revocation to be effective, the intent of the testator, whether express or implied, must be clear, and an act of revocation consistent with this intent must occur. Persons who wish to revoke a **Will** may use a codicil, which is a document that changes, revokes, or amends part or all of a validly executed **Will**. When a person executes a codicil that revokes some provisions of a previous **Will**, the courts will recognize this as a valid revocation. Likewise, a new **Will** that completely revokes an earlier **Will** indicates the testator's intent to revoke the **Will**.

Statements made by a person at or near the time that he/she intentionally destroys his/her **Will** by burning, mutilating, or tearing it clearly demonstrate his/her intent to revoke.

Sometimes revocation occurs by operation of law, as in the case of a marriage, divorce, birth of a child, or the sale of property devised in the **Will**, which automatically changes the legal duties of the testator. Many states provide that when a testator and spouse have been divorced but the testator's **Will** has not been revised since the change in marital status, any disposition to the former spouse is revoked.

6. Protection of the Family

The desire of society to protect the female spouse and children of a decendent is a major reason, both for allowing testamentary disposition of property and for placing limitations upon the freedom of testators.

Surviving Spouse: Three statutory approaches have developed to protect the surviving against disinheritance: Dower or Curtesy, the elective share, and Community Property.

Dower or Curtesy: At common law, a wife was entitled to dower, a life interest in one-third of the land owned by her husband during the marriage. Curtesy was the right of a husband to a life interest in all of his wife's lands. Most states have abolished common-law dower and curtesy and have enacted laws that treat husband and wife identically. Some statutes subject dower and curtesy to payment of debts, and others extend rights to personal property as well as land. Some states allow dower or curtesy in addition to testamentary provisions, though in other states dower and curtesy are in lieu of testamentary provisions.

Elective share: Although a testator can dispose of his/her property as he/she wishes, the law recognizes that the surviving spouse, who has usually contributed to the accumulation of property during the marriage, is entitled to a share in the property.

Otherwise, that spouse might ultimately become dependent on the state. For this reason, elective share was created by statue in states that do not have community property.

Most states have statutes allowing a surviving spouse to elect either a statutory share (usually one-third of the estate if children survive, one-half otherwise), which is the share that the spouse would have received if the decedent had died intestate, or the provision made in the spouse's **Will**. As a general rule, surviving spouses are prohibited from taking their elective share if they unjustly engaged in desertion or committed bigamy.

A spouse can usually waive, release, or contract away his/her statutory rights to an elective share or to dower or curtesy by either an antenuptial (also called prenuptial) or postnuptial agreement, if it is fair and made with knowledge of all relevant facts. Such agreements must be in writing.

Community property: A community property system generally treats the husband and wife as co-owners of property acquired by either of them during the marriage. On the death of one, the survivor is entitled to one-half of the property, and the remainder passes according to the **Will** of the decedent.

Children: Generally parents can completely disinherit their children. A court will uphold such provisions if the testator specifically mentions in the **Will** that he/she is intentionally disinheriting certain named children. Many states, however, have pretermitted heir provisions, which give children born or adopted after the execution of the **Will** and not mentioned in it an intestate share, unless the omission appears to be intentional.

Personal Guardians for Minor Children: If both parents die, the law requires that minor children have a personal guardian who can assume "parental duties" for the children. If no guardian is appointed through a **Will** or standalone legal document (other than a **Trust**), either a friend or relative may request guardianship from a court, or the court will choose the guardian; usually this is the nearest adult relative.

Property Guardians for Minor Children: While a personal guardian assumes the parental guidance of minor children, it is a **property guardian** who manages property left to children. The law states that children under eighteen cannot legally own more than a minimum amount of property without adult supervision. The person who takes responsibility for managing all property above that minimum amount for the benefit of the children is known as the property guardian. Often, the property guardian and the personal guardian are the same person, but this does not always have to be the case. A property guardian is also named through a **Will** or standalone document (other than a **Trust**.

7. Other Limitations on Will Provisions

The law has made other exceptions to the general rule that a testator has the un-qualified right to dispose of his/her estate in any way that he/she sees fit.

Charitable Gifts: Many state statutes protect a testator's family from disinheritance by limiting the testator's power to make charitable gifts. Such limitations are usually operative only where close relatives, such as children, grandchildren, parents, and spouse survive.

Charitable gifts are limited in certain ways. For example, the amount of the gift can be limited to a certain proportion of the estate, usually fifty percent. Some states prohibit deathbed gifts to charity by invalidating gifts that a testator makes within a specified period before death.

Ademption and Abatement: Ademption is where a person makes a declaration in his/her **Will** to leave some property to another and then reneges on the declaration, either by changing the property or removing it from the estate. Abatement is the process of determining the order in which property in the estate will be applied to the payment of debts, taxes, and expenses.

The gifts that a person is to receive under a **Will** are usually classified according to their nature for purposes of ademption and abatement. A specific bequest is a gift of a particular identifiable item of personal property, such as an antique violin, whereas a specific devise is an identifiable gift or real property, such as a specifically designated farm.

A demonstrative bequest is a gift of a certain amount of property---$2,000, for example---out of a certain fund or identifiable source of property, such as a savings account at a particular bank.

A general bequest is a gift of property payable from the general assets of the testator's estate, such as a gift or $5000.

A residuary gift is a gift of the remaining portion of the estate after the satisfaction of other dispositions.

When specific devises and bequests are no longer in the estate or have been substantially changed in character at the time of the testator's death, this is called ademption by extinction, and it occurs irrespective of the testator's intent. If a testator specifically provides in his/her **Will** that the beneficiary will receive his/her gold watch, but the watch is stolen prior to his/her death, the gift adeems and the beneficiary is not entitled to anything, including any insurance payments made to the estate as reimbursement for the loss of the watch.

Ademption by satisfaction occurs when the testator, during his lifetime, gives to his intended beneficiary all or part of a gift that he had intended to give the beneficiary in her **Will**. The intention of the testator is an essential element. Ademption by satisfaction applies to general as well as specific legacies. If the subject matter of a gift made during the lifetime of a testator is the same as that specified in a testamentary provision, it is presumed that the gift is in lieu of the testamentary gift where there is a parent-child or grandparent-parent relationship.

In the abatement process, the intention of the testator, if expressed in the **Will**, governs the order in which property will abate to pay taxes, debts, and expenses. Where the **Will** is silent, the following order is usually applied: residuary gifts, general bequests, demonstrative bequests, and specific bequests and devises.

CHAPTER FIVE

AN INTRODUCTION TO TRUSTS

General Definition of Trusts: A relationship created at the direction of an individual, in which one or more persons hold the individual's property subject to certain duties to use and protect it for the benefit of others.

Individuals may control the distribution of their property during their lives or after their deaths through the use of a **Trust**. There are many types of **Trusts** and many purposes for their creation. A **Trust** may be created for the financial benefit of the person creating the **Trust**, a surviving spouse or minor children, or a charitable purpose. Though a variety of **Trusts** are permitted by law, **Trust** arrangements that are attempts to evade creditors or lawful responsibilities will be declared void by the courts.

The law of **Trusts** is voluminous and often complicated, but generally it is concerned with whether a **Trust** has been created, whether it is a public or private **Trust**, whether it is legal, and whether the trustee has lawfully managed the **Trust** and **Trust** property.

1. Basic Concepts

The person who creates the **Trust** is the settlor. The person who holds the property for another's benefit is the trustee. The person who is benefited by the **Trust** is the beneficiary. The property that comprises the **Trust** is the trust res, corpus, principal, or subject matter. For example, a parent signs over certain stock to a bank to manage for a child, with instructions to give the dividend checks to him each year until he becomes twenty-one years of age, at which time he is to receive all the stock. The parent is the settlor, the bank is the trustee, the stock is the trust res, and the child is the beneficiary.

A fiduciary relationship exists in the law of **Trusts** whenever the settler relies on the trustee and places special confidence in her. The trustee must act in "Good Faith" with strict honesty and due regard to protect and serve the interests of the beneficiaries. The trustee also has a fiduciary relationship with the beneficiaries of the **Trust**.

A trustee takes legal title to the trust res, which means that the trustee's interest in the property appears to be one of complete ownership and possession, but the trustee does not have the right to receive any benefits from the property. The right to benefit from the property, known as equitable title, belongs to the beneficiary.

The terms of the **Trust** are the duties and powers of the trustee and the rights of the beneficiary conferred by the settlor when he/she created the **Trust**.

State statutes and court decisions govern the law of **Trusts**. The validity of a **Trust** of Real Property is determined by the law of the state where the property is located. The law of the state of the permanent residence (domicile) of the settlor frequently governs a **Trust** of Personal Property, but courts also consider a number of factors---such as the intention of the settlor, the state where the settlor lives, the state where the trustee lives, and the location of the **Trust** property---when deciding which state has the greatest interest in regulating the **Trust** property.

As a general rule, personal property can be held in a **Trust** created orally. Express

Trusts of real property, however, must be in writing to be enforced. When a person creates a **Trust** in his **Will**, the resulting testamentary **Trust** will be valid only if the **Will** conforms to the requirements of state law for **Wills**. Some states have adopted all or part of the Uniform Probate Code, which governs both **Wills** and testamentary **Trusts**.

2. Private Trusts

An express **Trust** is created when the settler expresses an intention either orally or in writing to establish the **Trust** and complies with the required formalities. An express **Trust** is what people usually mean when they refer to a **Trust**.

Every private **Trust** consists of four distinct elements: an intention of the settlor to create the **Trust**, a res or subject matter, a trustee, and a beneficiary. Unless these elements are present, a court cannot enforce an arrangement as a **Trust**.

Intention: The settlor must intend to impose enforceable duties on a trustee to deal with the property for the benefit of another. Intent can be demonstrated by words, conduct, or both. It is immaterial whether the word **Trust** is used in the **Trust** document. Sometimes, however, the words used by the settlor are equivocal and there is doubt whether the settlor intended to create a **Trust**. If the settlor uses words that express merely the desire to do something, such as the terms desire, wish, or hope, these precatory words (words expressing a wish) may create a moral obligation, but they do not create a legal one. In this situation a court will consider the entire document and the circumstances of the person who attempted to create the **Trust** to determine whether a **Trust** should be established.

The settlor must intend create a present **Trust**. Demonstrating an intent to create a **Trust** in the future is legally ineffective. When a settlor does not immediately designate the beneficiary, the trustee, or the **Trust** property, a **Trust** is not created until the designations are made.

Res or Subject Matter: An essential element of every **Trust** is the **Trust** property or res. Property must exist and be definite or definitely ascertainable at the time the **Trust** Is created and throughout its existence. Although stocks, bonds, and deeds are the most common types of **Trust** property, any property interest that can be freely transferred by the settler can be held in **Trust**, including Patents, copyrights, and Trademarks. A mere expectancy---the anticipation of receiving a gift by **Will**, for example---cannot be held in **Trust** for another because no property interest exists at that time.

If the subject matter of a **Trust** is totally destroyed, the **Trust** ends. The beneficiary might have a claim against the trustee for breach of **Trust**, however, if the trustee was negligent in failing to insure the **Trust** property. If insurance proceeds are paid as a result of the destruction, the **Trust** should be administered from them.

Trustee: Any person who has the legal capacity to take, hold, and administer property for his/her own use can take, hold, and administer property in **Trust**. Nonresidents of the state in which the **Trust** is to be administered can be trustees. State law determines whether an alien can act as a trustee. A corporation can act as a trustee. For example, a **Trust** company is a bank that has been named by a settlor to act as trustee in managing a **Trust**. A partnership can serve as a trustee if state law permits. An unincorporated association, such as a Labor Union or social club, usually cannot serve as a trustee.

The United States, a state, or a Municipal Corporation can take and hold property as trustee. This arrangement usually occurs when a settlor creates a **Trust** for the benefit of a military academy or a state college, or when the settler sets aside property as a park for the community.

The failure of a settlor to name a trustee does not void a **Trust**. The court appoints a trustee to administer the **Trust** and orders the person having legal title to the property to convey it to the appointed trustee.

If two or more trustees are appointed, they always hold the title to **Trust** property in Joint Tenancy with the Right of Survivorship. If one joint tenant dies, the surviving joint tenant inherits the entire interest, not just his/her proportionate share.

A trustee cannot resign without the permission of the court unless the **Trust** instrument so provides or unless all of the beneficiaries who are legally capable to do so consent to the resignation. The court usually permits the trustee to resign if continuing to serve will be an unreasonable burden for the trustee and the resignation will not be greatly detrimental to the **Trust**.

The removal of a trustee is within the discretion of the court. A trustee can be removed for habitual drunkenness, dishonesty, incompetency in handling **Trust** property, or the dissipation of the trustee estate. Mere friction or incompatibility between the trustee and the beneficiary is insufficient, however, to justify removal unless it endangers the Trust property or makes the accomplishment of the **Trust** impossible.

Beneficiary: Every private **Trust** must have a designated beneficiary or one so described that his/her identity can be learned when the **Trust** is created or within the time limit of the **Rule against Perpetuities**, which is usually measured by the life of a person alive or conceived at the time the **Trust** is created plus twenty-one years. This **Rule of Law**, which varies from state to state, is designed to prevent a person from tying up property in a **Trust** for an unlimited number of years.

A person or corporation legally capable of taking and holding legal title to property can be a beneficiary of a **Trust**. Partnerships and unincorporated associations can also be beneficiaries. Unless restricted by law, **Aliens** can also be beneficiaries.

A class of persons can be named the beneficiary of a **Trust** as long as the class is definite or definitely ascertainable. If property is left in **Trust** for "my children," the class is definite and the **Trust** is valid. When a **Trust** is designated "for my family," the validity of the **Trust** depends on whether the court construes the term to mean immediate family---in which case the class is definite---or all relations. If the latter is meant, the **Trust** will fail because the class is indefinite.

When an ascertainable class exists, a settlor may grant the trustee the right to select beneficiaries from that class. However, a **Trust** created for the benefit of any person selected by the trustee is not enforceable.

If the settlor's designation of an individual beneficiary or a class of beneficiaries is so vague or indefinite that the individual or group cannot be determined with reasonable clarity, the **Trust** will fail.

The beneficiaries of a **Trust** hold their equitable interest as tenants in common unless the **Trust** instrument provides that they shall hold as joint tenants. For example, three beneficiaries each own an undivided one-third of the equitable title in the **Trust** property. If they take as tenants in common, upon their deaths their heirs will inherit their proportionate shares. If, however, the settlor specified in the **Trust** document that they are to take as joint tenants, then upon the death of one, the two beneficiaries will divide his share. Upon the death of one of the remaining two, the lone survivor will enjoy the complete benefits of the **Trust**.

3. Creation of Express Trusts

To create an **Express Trust**, the settlor must own or have **Power of Attorney** over the property that is to become the **Trust** property or must have the power to create such property. The settlor must be legally competent to create a **Trust**.

A **Trust** cannot be created for an illegal purpose, such as to defraud creditors or to deprive a spouse of her rightful elective share. The purpose of a **Trust** is considered illegal when it is aimed at accomplishing objectives contrary to public policy. For example, a **Trust** provision that encourages **Divorce**, prevents a marriage, or violates the rule against perpetuities generally will not be enforced.

If the illegal provision pertains to the whole **Trust**, the **Trust** fails in its entirety. If, however, it does not affect the entire **Trust**, only the illegal provision is stricken, and the **Trust** is given effect without it.

4. Methods of Creation

A **Trust** may be created by an express declaration of **Trust**, a transfer in trust made either during a settlor's lifetime or under her will, an exercise of the power of appointment, a contractual arrangement, or statue. The method used for creating the **Trust** depends on the relationship of the settlor to the property interest that is to constitute the **Trust** property.

Declaration of Trust: A **Trust** is created by a declaration of **Trust** when the owner of property announces that she holds it as a trustee for the benefit of another. There is no need for a transfer because the trustee already has legal title. An oral declaration is usually sufficient to transfer equitable title to personal property, but a written declaration is usually required with respect to real property.

Trust Transfers: A **Trust** is created when property is transferred in **Trust** to a trustee for the benefit of another or even for the benefit of the settlor. Legal title passes to the trustee, and the beneficiary receives equitable title in the property. The settlor has no remaining interest in the property. A transfer in **Trust** can be executed by a deed or some other arrangement during the settlor's lifetime. This is known as an inter vivos **Trust** or living **Trust**.

Powers of Appointment: A power of appointment is the right that one person, called the donor, gives in a deed or a **Will** to another, the donee, to "appoint" or select individuals, the appointees, who should benefit from the donor's **Will**, deed, or **Trust**.

A person holding a general power of appointment can create a **Trust** according to the donor's direction by appointing a person as trustee to hold the **Trust** property for anyone, including herself or her estate. If that person holds a special power of appointment, she cannot appoint herself.

Contracts: Trusts can be created by various types of contractual arrangements. For example, a person can take out a life insurance policy on his/her own life and pay the premiums on the policy.

The insurer, in return, promises to pay the proceeds of the policy to an individual who is to act as a trustee for an individual named by the insured. The trustee is given the duty to support the beneficiary of this **Trust** from the proceeds during the beneficiary's life. The insured as settlor creates a **Trust** by entering into a contract with the insurance company in favor of a trustee. The **Trust** called an insurance **Trust**, is created when the insurance company issues its policy.

Statute: Statutes provide for the creation of **Trusts** in various instances. In the case of **Wrongful Death**, statutes often provide that a right of action exists in the surviving spouse or executor or administrator of the decedent with any recovery held in **Trust** for the designated beneficiaries.

5. Protection of Beneficiary's Interest from Creditors

Various **Trust** devices have been developed to protect a beneficiary's interest from creditors. The most common are spendthrift **Trusts**, discretionary **Trusts**, and support **Trusts**. Such devices safeguard the **Trust** property while the trustee retains it. Once funds have been paid to the beneficiary, however, any attempt at imposing restraint on the transferability of his/her interest is invalid.

Spendthrift Trusts: A **Spendthrift Trust** is one in which, because of either a direction of the settlor or statute, the beneficiary is unable to transfer his/her right to future payments of income or capital, and creditors are unable to obtain the beneficiary's interest in future distributions from the **Trust** for the payment of debts. Such **Trusts** are ordinarily created with the aim of providing a fund for the maintenance of another, known as the spendthrift, while at the same time protecting the **Trust** against the beneficiary's shortsightedness, extravagance, and inability to manage his/her financial affairs. Such **Trusts** do not restrict creditors' rights to the property after the beneficiary receives it, but the creditors cannot compel the trustee to pay them directly. The majority of states authorize spendthrift **Trusts**. Those that do not will void such provisions so that the beneficiary can transfer his/her rights and creditors can reach the right to future income.

Discretionary Trusts: A **Discretionary Trust** authorizes the trustee to pay to the beneficiary only as much of the income or capital of the **Trust** as the trustee sees fit to use for that purpose, with the remaining income or capital reserved for another purpose. This discretion allows the trustee to give the beneficiary some benefits under the **Trust** or to give her nothing. The beneficiary cannot force the trustee to use any of the **Trust** property for the beneficiary's benefit. Such a **Trust** gives the beneficiary no interest that can be transferred or reached by creditors until the trustee has decided to pay or apply some of the **Trust** property for the beneficiary.

6. Charitable Trusts

The purpose of a **Charitable Trust** is to accomplish a substantial social benefit for some portion of the public. The law favors charitable **Trusts** by according them certain privileges, such as an advantageous tax status. Before a court will enforce a charitable **Trust**, however, it must examine the alleged charity and evaluate its social benefits. The court cannot rely on the settlor's view that the **Trust** is charitable.

To be valid, a charitable **Trust** must meet certain requirements. The settlor must have the intent to create a charitable **Trust**, there must be a trustee to administer the **Trust**, which consists of some **Trust** property, and the charitable purpose must be expressly designated. The beneficiary must be a definite segment of the community composed of indefinite persons. Selected persons within the class must actually receive the benefit. The requirements of intention, trustee, and res in a charitable **Trust** are the same as those in a private **Trust**.

Charitable Purpose: A charitable purpose is one that benefits, improves, or uplifts humankind mentally, morally, or physically. The relief of poverty, the improvement of government, and the advancement of religion, education, or health are some examples of charitable purposes.

Beneficiaries: The class to be benefited in a charitable **Trust** must be a definite segment of the public. It must be large enough so that the community in general is affected and has an interest in the enforcement of the **Trust**, yet it must not include the entire human race. Within the class, however, the specific persons to benefit must be indefinite. A **Trust** "for the benefit of orphans of veterans of the 1991 Gulf War" is charitable because the class or category of beneficiaries is definite. The indefinite persons within the class are the individuals ultimately selected by the trustee to receive the provided benefit.

A **Trust** for designated persons or a **Trust** for profit cannot be a charitable **Trust**. A **Trust** to "erect and maintain a hospital" might be charitable even though the hospital charges the patients who are served, provided that any profits are used solely to continue the charitable services of the hospital.

As a general rule, a charitable **Trust** may last forever, unlike a private **Trust**. In a private **Trust**, the designated beneficiary is the proper person to enforce the **Trust**. In a charitable **Trust**, the state attorney general, who represents the public interest, is the proper person to enforce the **Trust**.

Cy Pres Doctrine: The doctrine of **Cy Pres**, taken from the phrase cy pres comme possible (French for "as near as possible"), refers to the power of a court to change administrative provisions in a charitable **Trust** when the settlor's directions hinder the trustee in accomplishing the **Trust** purpose. A court also has the power under the cy pres doctrine to order the **Trust funds** to be applied to a charitable purpose other than the one named by the settlor. This will occur if it has become impossible, impractical, or inexpedient to accomplish the settlor's charitable purpose. Because a charitable **Trust** can last forever, many purposes become obsolete because of changing economic, social, political, or other conditions. For example, a **Trust** created in 1930 to combat smallpox would be of little practical value today because medical advances have virtually eliminated the disease. When the cy pres doctrine is applied, the court reasons that the settlor would have wanted her general charitable purposes implemented despite the changing conditions.

The cy pres doctrine can be applied only by a court, never by the trustees of the **Trust**, who must execute the terms of the **Trust**. Trustees can apply to the court, however, for cy pres instructions when they believe that the **Trust** arrangements warrant it.

7. <u>Management</u>

The terms of a **Trust** instrument, when a writing is required, or the statements of a settlor, when she creates a **Trust**, set specific powers or duties that the trustee has in administering the **Trust** property. These express powers, which are unequivocal and directly granted to the trustee, frequently consist of the power to sell the original **Trust** property, invest the proceeds of any property sold, and collect the income of the **Trust** property and pay it to the beneficiaries. The trustee also has implied powers that the settlor is deemed to have intended because they are necessary to fulfill the purposes of the **Trust**.

A settlor can order the trustee to perform a certain act during the administration of the **Trust**, such as selling **Trust** realty as soon as possible and investing the proceeds in bonds. This power to sell is a mandatory or an imperative power. If the trustee fails to execute this power, he/she has committed a breach of **Trust**. The beneficiary can obtain a court order compelling the trustee to perform the act, or the court can order the trustee to pay damages for delaying or failing to use the power. The court can also remove the trustee and appoint one who will exercise the power.

Courts usually will not set aside the decision of a trustee as long as the trustee made the decision in good faith after considering the settlor's intended purpose of the **Trust** and circumstances of the beneficiaries. A court will not tell a trustee how to exercise his/her discretionary powers. It will only direct the trustee to use his/her own judgment. If, however, the trustee refuses to do so or does so in bad faith or arbitrarily, a beneficiary can seek court intervention.

A trustee, as a fiduciary, must administer the **Trust** with the skill and prudence that any reasonable and careful person would use in conducting her own financial affairs. The trustee's actions must conform to the **Trust** purposes. Failure to act in this manner will render a trustee liable for breach of **Trust**, regardless of whether she acted in good faith.

A trustee must be loyal to the beneficiaries, administering the **Trust** solely for their benefit and to the exclusion of any considerations of personal profit or advantage. A trustee would violate her fiduciary duty and demonstrate a conflict of interest if, for example, she sold **Trust** property to herself.

A trustee has the duty to defend the **Trust** and the interests of the beneficiaries against baseless claims that the **Trust** is invalid. If the claim is valid, however, and it would be useless to defend against such a challenge, the trustee should accede to the claim to avoid any unnecessary waste of property.

Trust property must be designated as such and segregated from a trustee's individual property and from property the trustee might hold in **Trust** for others. This requirement enables a trustee to properly maintain the property and allows the beneficiary to easily trace it in the event of the trustee's death or insolvency.

Generally, a trustee is directed to collect and distribute income and has the duty to invest the **Trust** property in income-producing assets as soon as is reasonable. This duty of investment is controlled by the settlor's directions in the **Trust** document, court orders, the consent of the beneficiaries, or statute. Some states have statutes that list various types of investments that a trustee may or must make. Such laws are known as legal list statutes.

One of the principal duties of a trustee is to make payments of income and distribute the **Trust** principal according to the terms of the **Trust**, unless otherwise directed by a court. Unless a settlor expressly reserves such power when creating the **Trust**, she cannot modify its payment provisions. In addition, the trustee cannot alter the terms of payment without obtaining approval of all the beneficiaries. Courts are empowered to permit the trustee to deviate from the **Trust** terms with respect to the time and the form of payment, but the relative size of the beneficiaries' interests cannot be changed. If a beneficiary is in dire need of funds, courts will accelerate the payment. This is called "hastening the enjoyment."

8. Revocation or Modification

The creation of a **Trust** is actually a conveyance of the settlor's property, usually as a gift. A **Trust** cannot be cancelled or set aside at the option of the settlor should the settlor change his/her mind or become dissatisfied with the **Trust**, unless the trust instrument so provides. If the settlor reserves the power to revoke or modify only in a particular manner, he/she can do so only in that manner. Otherwise, the revocation or modification can be accomplished in any manner that sufficiently demonstrates the settlor's intention to revoke or modify.

9. Termination

The period of time for which a **Trust** to operate is usually expressly prescribed in the **Trust** instrument. A settlor can state that the **Trust** shall last until the beneficiary reaches a particular age or until the beneficiary marries. When this period expires, the **Trust** ends.

When the duration of a **Trust** is not expressly fixed, the basic rule is that a **Trust** will last no longer than necessary for the accomplishment of its purpose. A **Trust** to educate a person's grandchildren would terminate when their education is completed. A **Trust** also concludes when its purposes become impossible or illegal.

When all the beneficiaries and the settlor join in applying to the court to have the **Trust** terminated, it will be ended even though the purposes that the settlor originally contemplated have not been accomplished. If the settlor does not join in the action, and if one or more of the purposes of the **Trust** can still be attained by continuing the **Trust**, the majority of U.S. courts refuse to grant a decree of termination. **Testamentary Trusts** cannot be terminated.

10. Creation of Trusts for Minor Children

While a guardian may not be named through a **Trust**, a **Trust** may be established to provide property itself for minor children. A **Trust** could be funded by life insurance policies on each parent's life. A **testamentary Trust** (a **Trust** that is created through a **Will**) allows parents to transfer assets to a trustee to manage for the benefit of the children. Conditions are set forth in the **Trust** under which the money is paid to the children, and the trustee has the authority to spend, sell, or invest the assets, all for the children's benefit. Any other properly drafted and funded revocable **Trust** accomplishes these same outcomes.

11. Other Estate Planning Procedures to Follow to Ensure that Minor Children as Beneficiaries Receive Designated Assets

NOTE: These Registration Procedures need to be implemented regardless of whether there is a **Trust, Will** or no **Will**. Of course, as you see in this Book, a **Trust** is the BEST option!

Transfer-On-Death (TOD): The Transfer-On-Death procedure is a way of designating beneficiaries to receive your assets at the time of your death without having to go through **Probate**. This designation also allows you to specify the percentage of assets each child/TOD beneficiary will receive. The Uniform Transfer-On-Death Securities Registation Act allows individuals to name someone to inherit stocks, bonds, brokerage accounts utilizing mutual funds, etc., without being subjected to the **Probate process.** There are also TOD bank accounts and TOD insurance policy accounts that operate in the same manner.

Joint Tenants with Right of Survivorship (JTWROS): Joint Tenants with Right of Survivorship is a type of brokerage account or bank account owned by at least two people, where all tenants have an equal right to the accounts assets and are afforded survivorship rights in the event of the death of the other account holder. In this type of brokerage or bank account, a surviving member will inherit the total value of the other member's share of account assets upon the death of that other member.

CHAPTER SIX

THE IMPORTANCE OF LIVING TRUSTS

1. WHAT IS A LIVING TRUST?

In the past, it was thought to be a good idea to have a **Will**, but today increasing numbers of people are discovering the advantages of having a **Living Trust** rather than a **Will**.

Most of us spend our lifetimes accumulating assets, but we give little or no thought to how, upon our death, our assets will be transferred to our heirs. We tend to assume that all of our personal assets, personal effects, business assets, insurance proceeds, and government benefits will go to our heirs. However, this presumption is false, according to a study conducted by the Estate Research Institute, a well-known organization doing extensive research and preparing professional publications in the area of estate planning. The Estate Research Institute's study indicates that 10% to 70% of a deceased person's assets will be used for the payment of probate fees, federal estate taxes, state inheritance taxes, and other associated costs!

Unfortunately, there exists misinformation, myths, and just plain old wives' tales on the topic of **Probate**. In fact, the majority of people do not even have **Wills**, and a great number who do have outdated ones.

You should know that the process of settling an estate through **Probate** can be costly, time-consuming, and frustrating. During **Probate**, stock values can deteriorate while the legal process moves forward with laborious and painful slowness; valuable businesses, built through years of hard work, can falter and die in the **Probate** process; small estates can be almost entirely consumed by legal fees. The tragedy is that none of this frustration process is necessary – with proper estate planning.

Any time and expense devoted to preplanning – that is, creating a **Living Trust** – are insignificant compared to the results of having done no planning. The cost for establishing a **Living Trust** varies. The creators of the **Living Trust** may establish a fee to be paid to the successor trustee for administering a **Trust** that is to exist for a lengthy period of time. At this point, the expenses associated with preplanning and administering your estate are realized at the beginning and are minimal – unless you fail to include assets in your **Living Trust** and then, those assets may be subject to **Probate**.

However, through the use of a **Will**, legal expenses are incurred whtn an attorney prepares your **Will**; statutory, extraordinary and reasonable fees are incurred to your estate upon your death and during the **Probate** process. The expenses associated with **Probate** are in addition to the human trauma of going through the **Probate** process.

The loss of a loved one is a devastating experience. It need not be made even more so by requiring the intervention of attorneys and accountants (in using the **Probate** process, when none is needed (with a **Living Trust**).

Perhaps most importantly, a revocable **Living Trust** eliminates the need to seek legal help, unless the survivor or trustee(s) feels better by doing so or assets have inadvertently been left outside the **Living Trust** and **Probate** of those assets is necessary. In fact, there is no need to have anyone get involved during this very personal and trying time, except those people whom the deceased would have wanted to be included.

2. PARTIES TO THE TRUST

We frequently play many roles simultaneously. A man may be a husband, father, doctor, and Little League coach; a woman may be a wife, mother, accountant, and Girl Scout leader. Each role is distinct and important. Similarly, when you have a **Living Trust**, you will generally serve as the trustor, the settlor, the trustee, and the beneficiary. Two other roles, distinct from the **Trust** be related to it, are the roles of the executor and the guardian. Since many of the legal terms associated with **Living Trusts** are not commonly understood, we will explain each of the terms identifying the parties to the **Trust**.

● Trustor/Trustmaker/Creator

The trustor/trustmaker is the individual or individuals who create the **Living Trust**. These individuals will sign the **Living Trust** as trustors/trustmakers (that is, the creators of the **Trust**). Having created and funded the **Trust**, the trustors/trustmakers have nothing further to do unless they wish to make a change to their **Trust**. The trustors/trustmakers will also sign any future amendments to the **Trust**.

● Settlor

The **settlor** (who is almost always the same individual or individuals as the trustors/trustmakers) is the individual or individuals who place the assets into the **Trust**. **Settlors** have absolute power over those assets, with the freedom to do as they wish with the assets until their death. The **settlors** may buy, sell, borrow against, and transfer the assets. The **settlors** also have the power to amend or revoke the **Trust** and to name the heirs.

The Settlor is sometimes referred to as the grantor, which is simply the Interanl Revenue Service name for the Settlor. **Grantor Trust** is the IRS name for a **Living Trust**.

● Trustee

The **trustee** is the individual or individuals who handle the administration of the **Trust**. When a **Trust** is initially created, the **trustees** are usually the same individuals as the trustors/trustmakers and settlors of the **Trust**. For a married couple usually husband and wife both act as **trustee**s.

You have presumably managed your assets reasonably well thus far, and this management should continue after you have created a **Living Trust**. Therefore, once your **Trust** is created, you will now step in as **trustee** of the **Trust** assets – with the same freedom and power to buy, sell, borrow against, or transfer the **Trust** assets as you had before creating a **Living Trust**.

• Surving Trustee

The **surviving trustee** is the individual who continues to manage the **Trust** after one of the original **trustees** has become deceased. Upon the death of one spouse, the surviving spouse most usually become the **surving trustee**, having the same freedom as before to manage the assets in the **Trust**.

• Successor Trustee

A **successor trustee** also must be named to succeed you as the manager of the **Trust** assets upon your death or imcompetence (if you are single) or upon the death or incompetence of both spouses (if you are married). This individual or individuals will take your place upon your death or imcompetence without requiring any court proceedings or legal action. The **successor trustee** will immediately have the same powers that you as trustee had to buy, sell, borrow against, and transfer the **Trust** assets – unless you choose to limit their powers. Another important function for the **successor trustee** is to use or distribute the assets as you have instructed in your **Living Trust**. However, a **successor trustee** may not in any way change the **Trust** (since he or she was not he creator of the **Trust**).

The **successor trustee's** job of administering a **Trust** requires little effort. Location of residence therefore need not be a factor in naming **successor trustees**. From time to time, decisions must be made and papers signed in order to buy, sell, transfer, or distribute assets within the **Trust**. Such decisions usually can be made fairly easily from one or many locations.

• More than One Successor Trustee

If you are concerned about who watches over the **trustee**, one way to alleviate your concerns is to appoint as **trustee** someone you trust. You can also obtain security in numbers by appointing **two or more trustees**. **Multiple trustees** will tend to monitor each other, so it is less likely that one of the **trustees** will do something that is not in the best interest of your estate.

If more that one **successor trustee** is named, all **successor trustees** must act together as co-trustees, unless you specify that you want the **successor trustees** to be able to act individually. Any action on behalf of the **Trust** will require the agreement and signature of each **sucessor co-trustee**.

- **Beneficiaries**

The surviving spouse is typically the **primary beneficiary** as well as the **surviving trustee**. The children or other named heirs are the **contingent beneficiaries**, meaning that they are **beneficiaries** only if they are living when the surviving spouse dies and assets are left in the **Trust** to be distributed to them.

Since the purpose of **Living Trust** for a married couple is to provide for the surviving spouse, the entire **Trust** may be used up to provide for the needs of the surving spouse. The only exception is that the **Decedent's Trust B** may be limited, such as by specifying "income only." Only after the surviving spouse's needs are fully satisfied will the children benefit from the **Trust**.

Upon the death of a parent (if single) or both parents (if married), the purpose of the **Trust** is to provide for the welfare of any minor children or handicapped children of any age or, where appropriate, any minor children of a deceased child.

3. <u>HOW DOES A LIVING TRUST WORK?</u>

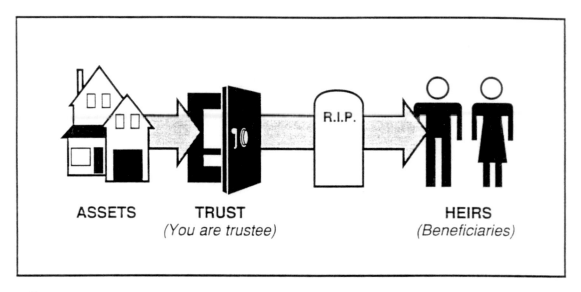

ASSETS

TRUST
(You are trustee)

R.I.P.

HEIRS
(Beneficiaries)

*J*ust like a Will, a Living Trust will enable you to control the distribution of your estate. It also enables you to reduce or avoid many of the fees and taxes that will be imposed upon your death.

A Living Trust also completely avoids Probate. Your estate will be available to your heirs immediately upon your death, without the delays or expensive court proceedings that accompany the Probate process.

What's a Trust?

A Trust is a legal arrangement under which one person or institution controls property given by another person for the benefit of a third party. The person giving the property is re-

ferred to as the trustor, the person controlling the property is referred to as the trustee, and the person for whom the trust operates is referred to as the beneficiary.

A Living Trust is simply a Trust that is established while you are still alive. A Trust that is established upon your death is called a "testamentary" Trust.

Before you panic at the thought of giving up control of your assets to a stranger, remember this: you are allowed to be the trustor - the person giving the property – and the trustee -- the person controlling the subsequent Trust. This means that you can maintain full control over all assets that you place into the Trust.

How Does It Work?

When you set up a Living Trust, you transfer ownership of all the assets you'd like to place in the Trust from you as an individual to yourself as trustee of the Trust. Legally, your Trust owns the assets with you as trustee. With the assets no longer in your personal name, there is nothing to Probate when you die.

And since you are the trustee, you maintain full control over the assets within the Trust. You can buy or sell as you see fit. You can even give assets away.

Trust have been in use for decades. And establishing a Trust is almost always less expensive that the alternative – going through Probate.

CHAPTER SEVEN

WHAT ARE MY OPTIONS (CHOICES)?

Generally, people do not like to think or talk about dying. But we all think about and plan for future things like: 1) retirement, 2) college education for ourselves, our children and our grandchildren, 3) starting our own business, 4) advancement of our careers, 5) getting out of debt, 6) the quality of our family's lives after we after we die and go to Heaven, etc.   So with these things in mind, what are we going to do in regard to Estate Planning ---**what are our Options (Choices)?**

Choice # 1…..Do Nothing

If you do nothing you will die intestate, which leaves your estate to be settled by the **Probate** Court. Over 70% of Americans die without a single piece of paper to say how they want their estate settled. Dying intestate guarantees **Probate**, with all of its costs, delays, and family heartaches (**the Pain and Suffering of Probate**).

Choice # 2…..Do a Will

A **Will** is nothing more than instructions to the **Probate** Court. It guarantees a trip to **Probate** where all your assets will be made public and anyone can contest your **Will** or make a claim against your estate. **Probate** can cost up to 10% of your estate's GROSS assets, and in some cases significantly more.

Choice # 3…..Do a Living Trust

A **Living Trust** completely eliminates **Probate** with all of its costs and delays. It will permit you to continue to have absolute management and control over your property/ assets until death or disability, at which time your successor trustee will follow your written instructions. Your assets will be transferred into your **Trust** now, at the time you establish your **Living Trust**, and this transfer is what avoids the **Probate** process. In addition to avoiding all of the expense, delay, trauma, and invasion of privacy caused by **Probate**, a **Living Trust** will provide for your care in the event of your incapacity without any court costs or attorney fees.

CHAPTER EIGHT

A SUMMARY OF THE PROBLEMS OF PROBATE

The Disadvantages of PROBATE:
(1) Excessive Fees and Expenses:
. Attorney Fees
. Executor Fees
. Probate Referee Fees
. Court Costs
. Extra Fees
. Accounting Fees
. Appraisal Fees
. Sales Commissions
. Bonds Premiums Expenses
(2) Excessive Delays – Distribution of Estate Property/Assets
(3) Loss of Control of Family Estate to **Probate** court
(4) No Privacy – Family Private Information Becoming Public Record
(5) Adverse Psychological Effects for Family Members
(6) Propensity for Law Suits Arising from Family Issues of Physical Violence
(7) Conservatorship/Guardianship Required by **Probate** Court for Health Issues
(8) Higher Estate Taxes

A Summary of the Problems of Probate:
- For the benefits of court supervision in **Probate**, your family will pay a heavy price:
1. EXCESSIVE FEES
   Attorney's fees, Executor's fees, Appraisal fees, Court filing fees and Bond Premiums
   are in some circumstances astronomical.
2. EXCESSIVE DELAYS
   Probate averages between six months and three years to complete depending on the
   complexity of the Estate. A reported national average is closing in on a two year delay
   average.
3. WHEN ARE ESTATE TAXES DUE?
   Within nine months of the death of a property owner.
4. WHAT IS PUBLIC RECORD?
   Probate records in most states reveal every detail of your family's financial life, and
   are available for public scrutiny at the County Courthouse. This may include names,
   addresses, phone numbers, and how much will be received.
5. WHAT IS THE PSYCHOLOGICAL IMPACT?
   Inflexible court proceedings are a constant reminder of the death of a family member.
   More often than not, heirs feel trapped, helpless, controlled and frustrated by Court
   actions.

6. WHAT ABOUT OUT OF STATE PROPERTY?

A **Will** requires **Probate**, with its accompanying legal and accounting fees, in every state where real estate is owned.

7. PROBATE FEES ARE BASED ON <u>GROSS</u> ESTATE

State law sets the **Probate** Fees that the attorneys and executors may charge. Many states allow attorneys to charge any reasonable fee, WITHOUT LIMITATION, to **Probate** a family's GROSS Estate. Also remember that **Probate** Fees can be levied on the death of EACH spouse when the decedent owns a certain minimum amount in real estate and personal property.

8. PROBLEM WITH COMMON DISASTER DEATHS

Spouses should be aware that in a **common disaster**, if one spouse survives the other, even by seconds, the surviving spouse will be the sole owner of joint tenant assets. This could have an adverse effect on intended heirs of both families. There are other reasons why Joint Tenancy is considered a very unwise way to hold title to major items of property. The first problem is that you have lost control of that property. It cannot be sold without the consent of the other joint tenants and could become liable for their debts and taxes. The biggest disadvantage of Joint Tenancy between spouses is that it can create huge capital gains tax liability of the surviving spouse.

9. ARE TAXES PAYABLE AT DEATH?

Yes, the **Probate** process puts a lien on the <u>ENTIRE ESTATE</u>!

In addition to the expense, delay and unwanted publicity of **Probate**, the family may also be liable for Federal Estate Taxes. When someone dies, the Federal Government levies a tax on his or her right to transfer assets to others. Taxes have a first lien on all Estates, Creditors have a second lien, and any remaining assets are distributed according to the **Will** to your designated heirs. The Federal Estate Tax is a substantial tax that effectively begins at a lower percentage and can reach a high percentage amount. The Federal Government has given every person in the United States an exemption of $1,000,000 for Estate Tax purposes. In deciding whether your Estate is greater than or less than the exempted amount, the Federal Government includes EVERYTHING you own, including the face value of your life insurance policies. Other Tax considerations include: State Inheritance Tax, Accrued State Income Tax, Accrued Federal Income Tax, Capital Gains Tax, and normally one year's Property Tax.

10. ESTATE VALUE DEPLETION FROM ESTATE TAXATION AND PROBATE FEES/COSTS

-- DEPLETED ESTATES OF FAMOUS PERSONS --

NAME	GROSS ESTATE	TOTAL SETTLEMENT	NET ESTATE	PERCENT SHRINKAGE
W. C. Fields	$884,680	$329,793	$554,887	37%
Franklin D. Roosevelt	1,940,999	574,867	1,366,132	30%
Humphrey Bogart	910,146	274,234	635,912	30%
Henry Kaiser, Sr.	5,597,772	2,488,364	3,109,408	44%
Al Jolson	4,385,143	1,349,066	3,036,077	31%
Gary Cooper	4,948,985	1,520,454	3,454,531	31%
Walt Disney	23,004,851	6,811,943	16,192,908	30%
Hedda Hopper	472,661	165,982	306,679	35%
Marilyn Monroe	819,176	448,750	370,426	55%
Cecil B. DeMille	4,043,607	1,396,064	2,647,543	35%
Elvis Presley	10,165,434	7,374,635	2,790,799	73%
J.P. Morgan	17,121,482	11,893,691	5,227,791	69%
John D. Rockefeller, Sr.	26,905,182	17,124,988	9,780,194	64%
Frederick Vanderbilt	76,838,530	42,846,112	33,992,418	56%

WALT DISNEY

FILM MAKER AND CREATOR OF DISNEY EMPIRE

GROSS ESTATE	**$**	**23,004,851**
TOTAL COSTS		**6,811,943**
NET ESTATE AFTER PROBATE	**$**	**16,192,908**

PROBATE EXPENSES

debts	$	2,022,055
administration fees		(unclear)
attorney's fee		150,000
executor's fee		125,000
state inheritance tax		771,428
federal estate tax		3,743,460
TOTAL PROBATE COSTS	$	6,811,943

OVER 29% REDUCTION OF ESTATE

CHAPTER NINE

'REAL LIFE' STORIES ABOUT PROBATE

(Stories about Pain and Suffering)

PLEASE NOTE: In God's eyes, we are all "special" to Him. In order to protect the privacy of the innocent, and to avoid incrimination of the guilty, certain names, times and places are withheld. The only exception is in the author, Rollie Riesberg's stories and Howard Hughes's story.

1. Special Person # 1 Stories (2)
(Rollie Riesberg)

(1978) Rollie's Dad's Death
(Part 1)

   The second hardest time of my life was when my dad died on July 28, 1978 of a sudden heart attack. My wife and I, our son, and my wife's parents were on vacation in the Hawaiian Islands. We were staying at a hotel in Kauai the night before we were to fly to Honolulu the next morning for a week's visit with my dad and stepmother, who lived in Kaneohe. (That evening, we got a telephone call from the pastor of my dad and stepmother's church telling us that my dad had passed away that day.) I was devastated---words cannot describe how very much I was hurting on the inside!! We caught the first flight to Honolulu early the next morning. My stepmother and stepsister met us at the airport. The first words out of my stepmother's mouth were: "You've killed your father! Why didn't you call him? He was worried sick over you!" You can imagine how I felt! I wanted to **die** and join my dad!!

   My stepmother was evading the truth: A couple of days before we left home to fly to Hawaii for our week-long vacation to the islands of Maui and Kauai and then to Honolulu for a week with Dad and my stepmother, I sent Dad and her a letter giving them our schedule and itinerary. (I also called Dad from California, when we were changing flights, to let him know _exactly_ what our vacation schedule was in the islands and when we would be arriving in Honolulu.) My wife's mom and dad (at my dad's invitation) were going to stay with Dad and my stepmother for two more weeks after Loretta, Doug and I left to return home to Atlanta. This was my dad's idea when he came to visit us and Loretta's parents for Christmas holiday seven months before he passed and went to Heaven. (This was the first time my dad came to visit us without bringing my stepmother with him; she opted to go to Guam to visit _her_ family for Christmas instead.) Anyway, Loretta's parents had _never_ been to Hawaii and my dad thought it would be a great treat for them to come to Hawaii with us and stay for 2 extra weeks so that he and my stepmother could give them the "Royal Treatment." I _purposely_ did _not_ call Dad and my stepmother once we arrived in Maui---I did _not_ want them to fly to Maui to join us because my stepmother, for the "Contol Freak" personality she had, would have <u>ruined</u> Loretta's parents' Hawaiian vacation. (My stepmother, two days after my dad died, informed me that she and Dad were planning on coming to Maui and Kauai to vacation with us!) I couldn't bring myself to tell my stepmother the **real** reason why I didn't call Dad and her from Maui, because it would have hurt her; and I did love her.

It took me over a year to get out of the "I don't want to live" mental mode---and my stepmother's statement to me, "You've killed your father." didn't help. Had it not been for my precious, loving wife and son's support, I probably would have died and joined my dad in Heaven; I knew Loretta and Doug needed me!

Three days after my dad died, Loretta and I went to visit my dad's best friend, who lived in the house immediately behind dad's house; he was so kind to tell Loretta and I what <u>really</u> caused my dad's death: That morning, the day Dad died, my stepmother Informed Dad that we were NOT going to stay with them when we came to visit with them the next day---**her** family members were coming to Honolulu and **THEY** were going to stay with them instead! Ending the BIG argument, my stepmother "stormed out of the house" and drove and was gone until late afternoon. My dad was "drinking heavily" while visiting with his best friend neighbor and spent all of the morning and most of the afternoon drinking and talking. His friend told him repeatedly that since he was taking strong blood pressure medicine, he shouldn't be drinking so much and should stop. Anyway, after drinking heavily all day, Dad walked home to get some more beer from the refrigerator---Dad was found lying on the floor in front of the refrigerator, dead from a massive heart attack. (My stepmother dealt with her own guilt by shifting it to <u>me</u>!)

To make matters worse, my dad died without a **Will** and all estate assets and property were held in Joint Tenancy with Right of Survivorship. The next day after my dad died, I noticed that my stepmother and stepsister were very busy "taking care of business." I discovered later on that what they were doing was moving most of the assets and real estate property into the Living Trust my stepmother's first husband left for her when he died in his late 30s. I was hurt even more since my dad didn't even remember me, his <u>only</u> child, or our son, his only blood-grandson, in any way. I asked my stepmother to give me dad's Daily Concordance Bible which he read to me and shared with me when he came to visit with us the December before he died; I also asked for his guitar and wrist watch---my stepmother refused! Years later, four years after my dad died, and a few years before my stepmother died, Loretta, Doug and I went to Hawaii to visit my stepmother; while there, I again asked her for my dad's bible and guitar. She said, "They are gone---the termites ate them!"

With this, my "word of advice" to you is: **DO NOT** take love and affection for granted! If you love someone, **tell** your love, **show** your love, and **do** your love---on a regular basis! And **do it** with a <u>**Living Trust**</u>!! Show your family you love them! Protect your estate assets for them! Protect them from the <u>**"Pain and Suffering"**</u> **of Probate!!**

(1978) Rollie's Dad's Death
(Part 2)

For about a year after my dad's passing, I didn't want to live---I wanted to die and join him in Heaven. With the help and prayers of my wife and son, and my church friends, Sunday School teacher and classmates, I was able to recover from my loss fairly well. Then by phone, I contacted a law firm of attorneys in Hawaii and paid $2,000 for them to conduct an investigation of my dad's estate situation. At the completion of their investigation, I was told that I could continue the project to attempt to get a settlement portion as the second heir to my dad's estate, but the legal costs would be extensive and the time period could be years. So, my wife and I decided that we couldn't go deeply in debt to pay exorbitant attorney fees and to wait for what could end of being many years for the estate settlement for me to be completed. So I gave up---without a fight! I was my dad's son and **only** child. My stepmother was the other heir to his estate. My mother, Mayme (Mae) was my dad's second wife; they were married from 1933 until 1942. I was 4 years old when they divorced in 1942. My stepmother was his third wife. My dad's first wife, whom he stayed married to for not even a year, was Garnet, the movie star, Gloria Swanson's best friend. They were all three born and raised in Minneapolis, Minnesota.

If my dad had have had a Living **Trust**, there wouldn't have been any problems for me or my stepmother or stepsister. And I know that my dad's estate was a **multi-million dollar estate**, because when rental property is owned in Hawaii, it makes it a multi-million dollar estate, automatically!

(2013) Rollie's Precious Wife, Loretta's Death

My precious little angel, Loretta, got cancer and died because of Satan and sin in the world. I thank God every day that she is no longer suffering because He rescued her from her cancer. She is now back home in Heaven, resting in peace, enjoying the ultimate happiness because she is with God, Jesus, her mom, dad, brother and grandparents. I have learned from going through this experience in my life that love, as created by God, is the BEST thing in the world, and a broken heart is the worst. As my broken heart is healing, I am growing closer and closer to God and Jesus. And I can't hardly wait until the day when I go to Heaven to be with Loretta, God and Jesus! But in the mean time, I still have a lot of work to do for God and Jesus, and writing this book to try to help you is a big part of that.

In 1992, Loretta and I purchased and established a Revocable Living **Trust** for ourselves and our family. I learned the **"hard way"** from my dad's passing how very important **Living Trusts** are in protecting family assets and property upon the death of a spouse. I wasn't about to put my wife and son through the "Pain and Suffering of **Probate**" that I experienced upon the death of my dad.

In 2013 when my precious Loretta passed, with our **Revocable Living Trust**, I didn't even have to speak to the **Probate** court, or do anything. We were both the settlors/grantors, trustees and beneficiaries. No lost money, time or anything. All I did is go to my attorney friend to get him to amend our **Living Trust** to add our son as co-trustee, and our son and grandsons as co-beneficiaries. And most important of all, we AVOIDED the "Pain and Suffering of **Probate**"!!

2. Special Person # 2 Story

My grandfather left my four siblings and myself five parcels of land in California. To pay their legal fees, the estate lawyer sold one of the properties. They told the realtor to sell it for $65,000 which is the amount they were owed.

They selected the parcel which was disconnected from the other four which probably seemed like a good idea to them. Unfortunately they sold the only parcel which was possible to subdivide. Subdivided into three, that parcel was worth about $330,000. The realtor sold the whole thing for $110,000 which was better than the $65,000 but much less than the $330,000 that the parcel was actually worth.

So we lost about $220,000 in probate there, not to mention the $65,000 in legal fees.

3. Special Person # 3 Story

I lost my mother at a young age, one year after my father had passed away. My mom had told me just a couple months before she passed away that she wanted to set up a **Living Trust**. She never completed that task and also did not have a simple **Will** prepared. After my mom passed away, an approximately two and a half year nightmare began for a college-age guy that knew nothing about **Probate**.

Her estate was very small and I had no legal access to any of her assets. I had to hire an attorney and start the **Probate** process. I was appointed independent administrator for her estate and had to set up a checking account in the name of the estate. While I was able to transfer her checking account funds to the new checking account, I was only allowed to use it for paying legal fees, which added up to an amount I could have never imagined.

Because she passed away without a **Will**, the state of Texas would be the institution that ultimately decided the fate of her estate, not my mother. I had to go through the painful process of dealing with creditors while they filed claims against the estate. I was told by my attorney that I could not pay them directly. Most of the creditors filed claims, as was required by the **Probate** court, except for one. That creditor, a large department store chain, made the choice to sue me directly, as independent administrator, instead of filing a proper claim through the **Probate** court. Again, I was told by the attorney that I could not pay them directly so as to not set a precedent for the other creditors. The credit card bill was originally $900. I ended up settling out of court for $250 and my bill from the attorney was over $5,000.

I had to hire a second attorney to represent the interest of any unknown heirs and had to go through a long process to prove that there were no other heirs. I also had to put my mom's home up for sale even though it was her desire for me to be able to keep it. There was no money available to me to be able to keep the house because of all the legal bills.

Throughout the process, I ended up having to pay the estate attorney over $17,000 in legal fees, which took most of my mom's small estate and legacy. I was not able to do anything to keep her dreams alive, a situation that would have veen very different if she had purchased a **Living Trust**. **Probate** was the most painful thing I have ever gone through in my life and I would not wish that pain on my worst enemy.

4. Special Person # 4 Story

My mother-in-law's health began to go the wrong direction probably a year and a half ago. She was looking at having a stint inserted. So she decided to write a **Will**, just in case. So, with the help of my wife they cobbled together a **Will**. It got signed and witnessed. This do-it-yourself project would come back to haunt us later.

Fast forward to October 2013. My mother-in-law goes into the hospital with breathing difficulties. The family has the expectation she will recover. From one day to the next her prognosis turns bad, real bad: as in life in a long term care facility on a ventilator for life. Thankfully, mother-in-law had both healthcare and financial powers of attorney in place. My wife served in both capacities. On October 21, 2013 my mother-in-law passed. Salt in the wound: money had to be borrowed to cremate the decedent!

The prospect of an estate and the possibility of inheriting assets does funny things to people. You find what your family members are really like at a time like this. In some it brings out the "vulture", greedy side of them. One family member even demanded to see the **Will** before his mother had passed! He continues to be a pain and promised to contest and tie up the **Will** in court as long as possible.

After visiting with two different attorneys on the matter, we settle on the second one. We were informed by both that the **Will** was incorrectly written. So, my mother-in-laws's home goes to **Probate**. Her other accounts were settled by virtue of joint accounts and beneficiary designations. My mother-in-law tried to divide the proceeds of those in the **Will**. Cannot be done! Those accounts will create tax consequences for the recipient!

Probate paperwork cost $2000 for openers. The attorney then gets paid out of the proceeds of the estate according to this schedule:

- 4% of the first $100,000
- 3% of the next $100,000
- 2% of the next $800,000
- 1% of the next 9,000,000
- 0.5% on the next $15,000,000
- A reasonable fee thereafter

Assuming the estate is liquid. In our case it may require selling the home! All of this assumes no one contests or the price goes up, way up. Try $350/hr. in attoreny fees!! We have probably a year of **Probate** pain to endure at this point, maybe more.

One more thing: When mom-in-law died we had to figure out what she was "on the hook" financially for things like ID theft protection, Medicare supplement, dental insurance, auto and homeowner insurance, retirement plan and so forth. My mother-in-law's strong suit was a heart for people NOT organization. So it took a lot of digging and phone calls to get things straightened out.

Bottom line: A **Will** is NOT a do-it-yourself project. Walking over dollars to pick up pennies by cobbling your own **Will** may have saved the decedent money, but will cost the remaining family members dearly, financially and emotionally.

My wife and I have a **Living Trust**. I tried to convince mom-in-law to buy a **Living Trust**. She said yes, but never came through. She mad excuses, put it off, and gave me "I'll get around to it". Too late now! ALL of this pain and expense could have been avoided with a **Living Trust**.

I now have a mission; I am determined to help as many people as I possibly can to see how important it is to have a **Living Trust** in their estate plan. When families buy a **Living Trust**, think of it as an act of love that will spare their loved ones misery like the one I have described above.

5. <u>Special Person # 5 Story</u>

My dad is dealing with **Probate** currently. His brother died at age eighty-seven with a **Will**. In the **Will** all tangible assets go to a niece, but all the money (intangibles) have no beneficiary, so according to the succession of family, my dad is the only living survivor of my uncle's family, he gets all the money. So Dad's niece has acquired a lawyer, and when he didn't give her the results she was looking for, she acquired a new lawyer which has held up the **Probate** process for three months now. There is nothing she can do to stop the money coming to my dad, because of the succession laws, but this has held up my dad receiving the money.

6. <u>Special Person # 6 Story</u>

My mother died of cancer at age forty-six without a **Living Trust**. **Probate** went on for over ten years and was never terminated. Because of **Probate**, we were forced to use estate monies to hire a **Probate** attorney in San Diego (where my mother died) and then later in Los Angeles (where I lived).

A **Living Trust** is a must for everyone. It saves the aggravation of **Probating** the estate which takes time and cost money, it saves money for some taxes charged to the beneficiaries, and it streamlines and efficiently carries out the wishes of the decedent. I can think of no reason <u>not</u> to have a **Living Trust**.

7. <u>Special Person # 7 Story</u>

My dear mom has passed and is now happily resting in peace in Heaven with my dad, our deceased family members, God and Jesus. She battled cancer and several other critical health problems for several years. I miss her so terribly much, but I am glad that she is no longer suffering . . . she suffered much too much, long and hard!!

Many years ago, my mom, in her **Last Will and Testament**, had designated that all family assets and property be given <u>equally</u> to all of her children. Much later on, because of my brothers and sisters extremely negative attitude and **total neglect** during her deeply sick and suffering last years, Mom decided to create another **Last Will and Testament**, leaving **<u>all</u>** family assets and property to **<u>me</u>**. Upon my mother's death, and my siblings findings that they had been disinherited in Mom's **last Will**, my brothers and sisters became physically violent to me! Additionally, they legally issued a "Restraining Order" and a "Class Action" law suit against me in order to try to circumvent the decree of our mother's **last Will**---all of this action was based on their **lies** against me.

Our mom's estate consisted of assets and property valued at millions of dollars. Years earlier, our mom's and dad's best friends, who didn't have any family heirs/relatives who were still alive, **Willed** their multi-million dollar estate to our mom and dad. Some years later, when our mom's and dad's best friends passed, our mom and dad inherited the entire multi-million dollar estate.

Because of my brothers and sisters **lies** about me, as told to law enforcement, legal and court officials, I have had to complete community services and anger management class assignments and pay exorbitant legal fees and fines. The truth-of-the-matter is that I <u>do not</u> tell lies and I was **<u>not</u>** lying. People are <u>not</u> supposed to be "framed" by close, immediate family members! I am "<u>living proof</u>" that "fighting-over-money" can bring out the <u>worst</u> character in people!

With all of the unresolved pending legal issues and disagreements on the part of my brothers and sisters, the Probate Court process has still **not** begun. And too, the **second** and **last Will** created by my mom, is now missing and **cannot be found**! Additionally, with all of these unresolved issues, all assets and property in our mom's estate are "frozen" and inaccessible to me and my brothers and sisters. These assets and property Include houses and land, investments and savings accounts, corporations stock ownership, personal belongings and checking accounts. Under these conditions, who knows how many years it will take for the **Probate** court process to begin and then eventually be completed. And too, how much estate money is going to be spent and **wasted** for attorney fees, **Probate** court costs and fees, housing and property appraisal fees, sales commissions, property and housing values depletion, etc. God only knows! No wonder there is so much "**Pain and Suffering with Probate!**"

8. Special Person # 8 Story

Having No Idea About Probate:

After finding out about my father's tumor in his lung, and it being cancer that had developed to a stage four, I put my job, my business commitments, and my personal life on hold and committed myself to taking care of my father! During my father's two year battle with this terrible disease, we continually discussed the matter of putting his house in my name. Unfortunately, I was not successful in doing so, because my father was too sick to want to discuss "decision-making" business matters like this. After my father's passing, I've discovered that in order to completely follow through with my father's **Last Will and Testament**, I will have to go to **Probate** Court, something I know nothing about. The more I learn about the **Probate** procedure and the deep financial loss that will be expected of me to endure, the more fear and anxiety builds up within me. Several years has done passed without me being able to respectively follow through and execute my father's **Will**. Financial costs and fear of losing the home my father finally left to me in his **Will**, is the reason why I haven't been able to start the **Probate** procedure!

If me and my father had only known about setting up the house and all of its equity in a **Living Trust** with his **Will**, then the whole **Probate** procedure and the fear and anxiety that accompanies it, would not be necessarily within me.

And I am praying every day that God will help me resolve this **Probate** issue with me still being able to keep my father's house, because I have to have a place to live. And I thank God for all of the wonderful memories of my father and I living there together during all of those years of my whole life!

When I finally represent myself and my father's **Last Will and Testament** in the **Probate** court, I pray it all goes well!! This is coming from me being a true believer in **God** and **Living Trusts!!**

9. Special Person # 9 Story

Howard Hughes and the Mormon Will

When billionaire recluse Howard Hughes died in 1976, it appeared that he had not left a **Will**. Attorneys and executives of Hughes's corporations began an intensive search to find a **Will**, while speculation grew that Hughes might have left a holographic (hand-written) **Will**. One attorney publicly stated that Hughes had asked him about the legality of a holographic **Will**.

Soon after the attorney made the statement, a holographic **Will** allegedly written by Hughes appeared on a desk in the Salt Lake City headquarters of the Church of Jesus Christ of Latter-day Saints, more commonly known as the Mormon Church. After a preliminary review, a document examiner concluded that the **Will** might have been written by Hughes. The Mormon Church then filed the **Will** in the county court in Las Vegas, Nevada, where Hughes's estate was being settled.

The **Will**, which became known as the **Mormon Will**, drew national attention for a provision that gave one-sixteenth of the estate, valued at $156 million, to Melvin Dummar, the owner of a small gas station in Willard, Utah. Dummar told reporters that in 1975 he had picked up a man who claimed to be Howard Hughes and had dropped him off in Las Vegas.

Though Dummar first said he had no prior knowledge of the **Will** or how it appeared at the church headquarters, he later claimed that a man drove to his service station and gave him the **Will** with instructions to deliver it to Salt Lake City. Dummar said he had destroyed the instructions.

Investigators discovered that Drummer had checked out a library copy of a book called The Hoax, which recounted the story of Clifford Irving's forgery of an "autobiography" of Hughes. The book contained examples of Hughes's handwriting. Document examiners demonstrated that Hughes's handwriting had changed before the time the **Mormon Will** supposedly was written. In addition, the examiners concluded that the **Will** was a crude forgery. Nevertheless, it took a seven-month trial and millions of dollars from the Hughes estate to prove that the **Will** was a fake. In the end, the court ruled that the **Will** was a forgery.

No valid **Will** was ever found. Dummar's story later became the subject of the 1980 motion picture *Melvin and Howard*.

CHAPTER TEN

BE KIND TO OTHERS---STRESS CAN KILL

Be kinder than necessary, for everyone you meet is fighting some kind of battle. Live simply, Love generously, Care deeply-----Leave the rest to God.

There is no definitive reason why we should say and do hurtful things to people. We may not know it but the person we are being verbally and emotionally abusive to may secretly love and admire us. Like I always say jokingly, "Be kind to everyone because you never know who is going to be your Boss some day."

Yes, stress can kill a person. Research shows that a weakened immune system can lead to cancer. A strong immune system seeks out and destroys cancer cells. Cancer cells are prevalent in everyone's body but a strongly healthy immune system will keep cancer cells in the body subdued.

In my search efforts to help the readers of this, my book has produced the following research results as compiled by the **National Cancer Institute:**

National Cancer Institute at the National Institutes of Health

Fact Sheet   (Revised: 12/10/2012)

Psychological Stress and Cancer

Key Points:

-Psychological stress alone has not been found to cause cancer, but psychological stress that lasts a long time may affect a person's overall health and ability to cope with cancer.

-People who are better able to cope with stress have a better quality of life while they are being treated for cancer, but they do not necessarily live longer.

1. What is psychological stress?

Psychological stress describes what people feel when they are under mental, physical, or emotional pressure. Although it is normal to experience some psychological stress from time to time, people who experience high levels of psychological stress or who experience it repeatedly over a long period of time may develop health problems (mental and/or physical).

Stress can be caused both by daily responsibilities and routine events, as well as by more unusual events, such as a trauma or illness in oneself or a close family member. When people feel that they are unable to manage or control changes caused by cancer or normal life activities, they are in distress. Distress has become increasingly recognized as a factor that can reduce the quality of life of cancer patients. There is even some evidence that extreme distress is associated with poorer clinical outcomes. Clinical guidelines are available to help doctors and nurses assess levels of distress and help patients manage it.

The fact sheet provides a general introduction to the stress that people may experience as they cope with cancer. More detailed information about specific psychological conditions related to stress can be found in the Related Resources and Selected References at the end of this fact sheet.

2. How does the body respond during stress?

The body responds to physical, mental, or emotional pressure by releasing stress hormones (such as epinephrine and norepinephrine) that increase blood pressure, speed heart rate, and raise blood sugar levels. These changes help a person act with greater strength and speed to escape a perceived threat.

Research has shown that people who experience intense and long-term (i.e. chronic) stress can have digestive problems, fertility problems, urinary problems, and a weakened immune system. People who experience chronic stress are also more prone to viral infections such as the flu or common cold and to have headaches, sleep trouble, depression, and anxiety.

3. Can psychological stress cause cancer?

Although stress can cause a number of physical health problems, the evidence that it can cause cancer is weak. Some studies have indicated a link between various psychological factors and an increased risk of developing cancer, but others have not.

Apparent links between psychological stress and cancer could arise in several ways. For example, people under stress may develop certain behaviors, such as smoking, overeating, or drinking alcohol, which increase a person's risk for cancer. Or someone who has a relative with cancer may have a higher risk for cancer because of a shared inherited risk factor, not because of the stress induced by the family member's diagnosis.

4. How does psychological stress affect people who have cancer?

People who have cancer may find the physical, emotional, and social effects of the disease to be stressful. Those who attempt to manage their stress with risky behaviors such as smoking or drinking alcohol or who become more sedentary may have a poorer quality of life after cancer treatment. In contrast, people who are able to use effective coping strategies to deal with stress, such as relaxation and stress management techniques, have been shown to have lower levels of depression, anxiety, and symptoms related to the cancer and its treatment. However, there is no evidence that successful management of psychological stress improves cancer survival.

Evidence from experimental studies does suggest that psychological stress can affect a tumor's ability to grow and spread. For example, some studies have shown that when mice bearing human tumors were kept confined or isolated from other mice—conditions that increase stress—their tumors were more likely to grow and spread (metastasize). In one set of experiments, tumors transplanted into the mammary fat pads of mice had much higher rates of spread to the lungs and lymph nodes if the mice were chronically stressed than if the mice were not stressed. Studies in mice and in human cancer cells grown in the laboratory have found that the stress hormone norepinephrine, part of the body's fight-or-flight response system, may promote angiogenesis and metastasis.

In another study, women with triple-negative breast cancer who had been treated with neoadjuvant chemotherapy were asked about their use of beta blockers, which are medications that interfere with certain stress hormones, before and during chemotherapy. Women who reported using beta blockers had a better chance of surviving their cancer treatment without a relapse than women who did not report beta blocker use. There was no difference between the groups, however, in terms of overall survival.

Although there is still no strong evidence that stress directly affects cancer outcomes, some data do suggest that patients can develop a sense of helplessness or hopelessness when stress becomes overwhelming. This response is associated with higher rates of death, although the mechanism for this outcome is unclear. It may be that people who feel helpless or hopeless do not seek treatment when they become ill, give up prematurely on or fail to adhere to potentially helpful therapy, engage in risky behaviors such as drug use, or do not maintain a healthy lifestyle, resulting in premature death.

5. How can people who have cancer learn to cope with psychological stress?

Emotional and social support can help patients learn to cope with psychological stress. Such support can reduce levels of depression, anxiety, and disease-and treatment-related symptoms among patients. Approaches can include the following:

• Training in relaxation, meditation, or stress management
• Counseling or talk therapy
• Cancer education sessions
• Social support in a group setting
• Medications for depression or anxiety
• Exercise

More information about how cancer patients can cope with stress can be found in the PDQ® summaries listed in the Related Resources section at the end of this fact sheet.

Some expert organizations recommend that all cancer patients be screened for distress early in the course of treatment. A number also recommend re-screening at critical points along the course of care. Health care providers can use a variety of screening tools, such as a distress scale or questionnaire, to gauge whether cancer patients need help managing their emotions or with other practical concerns. Patients who show moderate to severe distress are typically referred to appropriate resources, such as a clinical health psychologist, social worker, chaplain, or psychiatrist.

Selected References

1. Atherholt SB, Fann JR. Psychosocial care in Cancer. *Current Psychiatry Reports* 2012;14(1): 23-29. [PubMed Abstract]
2. Fashoyin-Aje LA, Martinez KA, Dy SM. New Patient-centered care standards from the Commission on Cancer; opportunities and challenges. *Journal of Supportive Oncology* 2012; e-pub ahead of print March 20, 2012. [PubMed Abstract]
3. Lutgendorf SK, DeGeest K. Dahmoush L, et al. Social isolation is associated with elevated tumor norepinephtine in ovarian carcinoma patients. *Brain, Behavior, and Immunity* 2011;25(2): 250-255. [PubMed Abstract]
4. Lutgendorf SK, Sood AK, Anderson B, et al. Social support, psychological distress, and natural killer cell activity in ovarian cancer. *Journal of Clinical Oncology* 2005:23(28):7105-7113 [PubMed Abstract]
5. Lutgendorf SK, Sood AK, Antoni MH. Host factors and cancer progression: biobehavioral signaling pathways and interventions. *Journal of Clinical Oncology* 2010;28(26):4094-4099. [PubMed Abstract]
6. McDonald PG, Antoni MH, Lutgendorf SK, etal. A biobehavioral perspective of tumor biology. *Discovery Medicine* 2005;5(30):520-526. [PubMed Abstract]
7. Melhem-Bertrandt A, Chavez-Macgreagor M, Lei X, et al. Beta-blocker use is associated with improved relapse-free survival in patients with triple-negative breast cancer. *Journal of Clincal Oncology* 2011;29(19):2645-2652. [PubMed Abstract]

8. Moreno-Smith M, Lutgendorf SK, Sood AK. Impact of stress on cancer metastasis. *Future Oncology* 2010;6(12):1863-1881. [PubMed Abstract]
9. Segerstrom SC, Miller GE. Psychological stress and the human immune system: a meta-analytic study of 30 years of inquiry. *Psychological Bulletin* 2004;130(4):601-630. [PubMed Abstract]
10. Sloan EK, Priceman SJ, Cox BF, et al. The sympathetic nervous system induces a metastatic switch in primary breast cancer. *Cancer Research* 2010;70(18):7042-7052. [PubMed Abstract]

CHAPTER ELEVEN

WHAT IS THE SOLUTION TO THE PROBLEMS?

As you, the readers of this very Important Book's previous Chapters have seen, the **Solution** to the **Problems of Probate** is in establishing a **Living Trust** for you and your family!

And **Timing is Everything**. None of us know when our time here on earth will be over, when God will bring us home to Heaven. We know you love your family and want the **BEST** for them---so establish a Living Trust **now**!

Turn to The Experts. There are Lawyers and Law Firm companies out there that specialize in the development of various types of Living Trusts for estate planning. When you need an EXPERT, go there! PLEASE NOTE, if you and your family need guidance in finding Living Trust EXPERTS, please Contact us on our Websites:

– Financial Growth Services –
www.financialgrowthservices.com
Email: fingrowserv@bellsouth.net
– LCR Estae Planning Services, LLC –
www.lcrestateplanningservices.com
Emails: rgriesberg@bellsouth.net
lcr.riesberg@bellsouth.net
R.G. (Rollie) Riesberg – Owner and Author

We, the Authors of this Book and our others, are "'People-Problem' Engineers of Life"

CHAPTER TWELVE

MAY YOU REST IN ULTIMATE PEACE AND HAPPINESS......FOREVER

1) God loves you and your family.

2) We love you and your family---and we want the BEST for you/your family.

3) A broken heart from the loss of a dear loved one is the worst thing in the world and God's LOVE for us and His gift of eternal salvation and life is the BEST!

4) With all of your thoughts about what is happening in your life, dwell on the good, happy things that are going on in your life...and learn to stay busy "counting your blessings!"

5) Goodbye Pain & Suffering of Probate!

PAIN and SUFFERING and DEATH STARTED WITH SATAN and ADAM and EVE

Satan: (Revelation 12: 7-9) 7 "Now war arose in heaven, Michael and his angels fighting against the dragon; and the dragon and his angels fought" 8 "but they were defeated and there was no longer any place for them in heaven." 9 "And the great dragon was thrown down, that ancient serpent, who is called the Devil and Satan, the deceiver of the whole world—he was thrown down to the earth, and his angels were thrown down with him."

   Satan/Lucifer/The Devil: (Ezekiel 28: 11-19) God created Satan as an Angel. Jesus calls him the ruler of the world. ˎSatan means adversary' or ˎenemy'.

Satan and Adam and Eve: (Revelation 12: 9) "There was the unholy presence of an enemy, Satan (the Devil) whose sole aim was to destroy God's creation including humanity. Appearing to Eve in the form of a serpent, the Devil twisted a clear command of God into a lie and led the first couple to distrust and disobey their Heavenly Father." (Genesis 3: 1-6) "Sin immediately entered the human experience, resulting in the curse of death falling on the entire creation."

Pain: (Revelation 16:10-11) 10 "The fifth angel poured his bowl on the throne of the beast, and its kingdom was in darkness ; men gnawed their tongues in anguish" 11 "and cursed the God of heaven for their pain and sores, and did not repent of their deeds." A broken heart is by far the worst pain of all.

Death: (Daniel 12:2) 2 "And many of those who sleep in the dust of earth shall awake, some to everlasting life, and some to shame and everlasting contempt." (Revelation 1:18) "Death held us in inescapable bondage, and the Devil was our master. However, when Jesus laid down his life on the cross and arose from the dead, He shattered death's power." (Revelation 20:10, 14-15) "In the end of time, Satan himself will spend eternity in the lake of fire in hell, along with death, the grave and all people who reject salvation in Jesus."

Pain and suffering and death comes to all of us because of sin and Satan in the world. But God loves us so much that He has implemented a rescue plan for us: He sent His Son, Jesus Christ to die for our sins, that we may have eternal life. Jesus died in our place and our sin debt has been paid-in-full by His blood on the cross. In heaven there will be no more sin, pain, suffering and death, and our sorrow will be gone forever! **Pray to God and thank Him!!!**

THE MOST DIFFICULT TIMES OF OUR LIVES

I cannot go on any longer.: (II Corinthians 12:9) And He said unto me, "My grace is sufficient for thee: for my strength is made perfect in weakness." Most gladly therefore will I rather glory in my infirmities, that the power of Christ may rest upon me. (Psalm 91:15) He shall call upon me, and I will answer him: I will be with him in trouble; I will deliver him, and honour him.

I feel alone.: (Hebrews 13:5) Let your conversation be without covetousness; and be content with such things as ye have: for he hath said, I will never leave thee, nor forsake thee.

I am discouraged.: (Psalm 46: 1) God is our refuge and strength, a very present help in trouble.

WHEN WE HAVE ARRIVED---COUNTING OUR BLESSINGS

Blessings: (Psalm 23) 1. The Lord is my shepherd; I shall not want. 2. He maketh me to lie down In green pastures: he leadeth me beside still waters. 3. He restoreth my soul: he leaded me in the paths of righteousness for his name's sake. 4. Yea, though I walk through the valley of the shadow of death, I will fear no evil: for thou art with me; thy rod and thy staff they comfort me. 5. Thou preparest a table before me in the presence of mine enemies: thou anointest my head with oil; my cup runneth over. 6. Surely goodness and mercy shall follow me all the days of my life: and I will dwell in the house of the Lord for ever. (Psalm 73:23) I am continually with thee; thou hast holden me by my right hand. 26. My flesh and my heart faileth: but God is the strength of my heart, and my portion for ever.

We will know that we have arrived at the place where God wants us to be for Him and ourselves when we start recognizing how good God has been to us and we start 'counting our blessings'. Life itself is one of those blessings! God wants us to use the blessings He has given us (our talents, our intelligence, our knowledge and our time) to His and our best advantage to the glory of His kingdom. And when we start sharing God's love for us, with others who are hurting from broken hearts from the loss of their dear loved ones and are suffering from deeply problematic times in their lives, we are doing what God has put us here on earth for. God is love! Love, as created by God, is the best thing on earth and a broken heart is the worst. Love is the reason for the season and always; love is all about Christmas and Christmas is all about love. God gave us His only begotten Son, Jesus Christ because He loves us so very much! And Jesus died on the cross for our sins, so that we may have eternal life, love and happiness in Heaven one day. If God loves us that much, then we all need to strive to love our wives and husbands as much and in the same way. I would have given my life for my precious Loretta and she would have done the same for me.

CHAPTER THIRTEEN

OUR TRIBUTE TO YOU.....HELPUL FINANCIAL INFORMATION

In this modern society in which we live these days, money and finances are very important! Without our jobs and money, our lives would be in "financial shambles!"

And without money, we cannot help ourselves, much less anyone else who is experiencing joblessness, homelessness, hunger, bad health, etc. And of course, when we lose our dear loved one, we must not let the **Probate** process take the money we have worked so hard to accumulate during our lives, and delay the settlement of our estate while we are so deeply grieving..........

Getting Started---CHARTING The Course for Your Financial Future (FINANCIAL GROWTH)

(Refer to Chart 1—Getting Your Financial House in Order)

PART 1—What You Need to Do NOW

Establish Goals (on paper with targeted dollar amounts) and start saving/ investing for each of those goals on a monthly basis. The following is a typical list of Goals in order of importance (first on list being most important):

(1) Establish an Emergency Fund

NOTE: This Fund is needed as a source for money to avoid having to charge or get a bank loan to pay for unexpected emergencies such as car breakdown, home roof leaking, job layoff, etc.; also, to accumulate money to pay cash for larger purchases.

(2)   Have adequate insurance protection for Health, Disability, Life, Homeowner's, Car and Long Term Care insurance.

(3) Develop a Budget for Living Expenses; and stay on budget.

(4) Establish a Retirement Plan

NOTES:

a) Take full advantage of your employer's 401(k), 403(b) or 457 Plan, as applicable, especially if there is matching by your employer up to a certain percentage of the dollar amount you contribute monthly.

b) Contribute the maximum yearly to your IRA (Roth or Traditional).

c) If you have a part time business in addition to your full time job, you can also have a Simple IRA, Roth or Single 401(k), or SEP account as long as the IRS maximum allowed annual contribution amount is not exceeded.

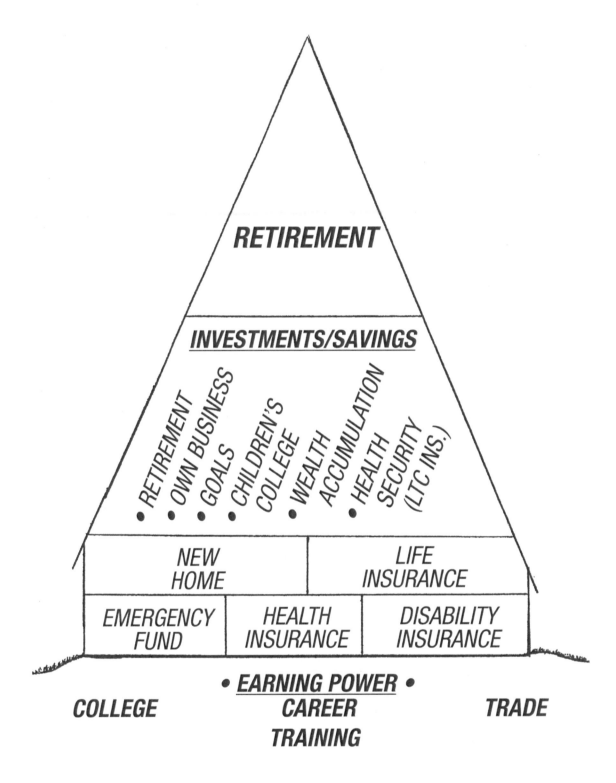

RETIREMENT

INVESTMENTS/SAVINGS

- RETIREMENT
- OWN BUSINESS
- GOALS
- CHILDREN'S COLLEGE
- WEALTH ACCUMULATION
- HEALTH SECURITY (LTC INS.)

NEW HOME	LIFE INSURANCE

EMERGENCY FUND	HEALTH INSURANCE	DISABILITY INSURANCE

• **EARNING POWER** •
CAREER TRAINING

COLLEGE   **TRADE**

<u>CHART 1</u>–Getting Your Financial House in Order   by Rollie Riesberg
Financial Growth Services

50

(5) Establish an Investment/Savings Plan for future Goals such as:

    1) New Home 2) Vacation Home

    3) Start a New Business 4) Career Change

    5) New Car and 6) Start a <u>Money Fund</u> for higher cost cash purchases.

(6) Establish an Investment/Savings Plan for your Children's College or Trade
    School expenses.

> **(Refer to <u>Money Charts 2 & 3</u> to see how hard Annual and Lump Sum invested money can work for you to help you achieve your monetary goals. These Charts are based on <u>Chart 4</u> -The Rule of 72 "Compounding Rule".)**

PART 2—Hard-Workin' Money Hints

> **(Refer to <u>Chart 5</u> to see when your Investment/Savings money works the hardest.)**

In our modern society, we can obtain money 4 ways:

    1) Work for money

    2) Let our money work for us

    3) Wait around until we inherit money (don't count on it)

    4) Accept charity (I don't think so).

PART 3-Ten Rules for Money Managemt.

> **(Refer to <u>Chart 6</u> to see how you can <u>best</u> manage your money and budget).**

These basic rules are guidelines for good, effective money management, whether it is for individual families, small businesses or corporations.

PART 4—What Affects the Stock Market

> **(Refer to <u>Chart 7</u> to see the things that can have a positive or negative effect on the Stock Market and stock prices in general.)**

In previous years, the main determinants for Stock Market conditions and levels were the Economy, Corporate Profits and Interest Rates/Inflation. In most recent years, Energy Prices and the Threat of Terrorism have become additional determinants, making the stock market puzzle more complex and
sometimes more perplexing.

PART 5—Why Wealthy People are Wealthy

> **(Refer to <u>Chart 8</u> to find the answers to this question.)**

It has often been said that many of the Wealthy people are not necessarily any smarter than most of the rest of us. But there are distinct reasons why they have become wealthy:

    1) They work harder.

    2) They take more chances and risks.

    3) They try more things and consequently, have more failures, but (this being a
       "numbers game") they also have more successes.

    4) They are more in tune with recognizing opportunities as they arise.

PART 6—Giving Back (Show His Love------Give)

(Refer to <u>Chart 9</u> to see how very blessed we <u>really</u> are and what God expects us to do with our lives.)

God expects us to give: 1) our money 2) our time and 3) our talents helping others who are in need and are not as fortunate as us.

$1,200 Year at Varying Rates Compounded Annually - End of Year Values

	5th Yr.	10th Yr.	15th Yr.	20th Yr.	25th Yr.	30th Yr.	35th Yr.	40th Yr.
1%	6,182	12,680	19,509	26,686	34,231	43,359	50,492	59,250
2%	6,369	13,402	21,168	29,739	39,205	49,654	61,192	73,932
3%	6,561	14,169	22,988	33,211	45,063	58,803	74,731	93,195
4%	6,760	14,983	24,990	37,162	51,974	69,993	91,917	118,592
5%	6,962	15,848	27,188	41,662	60,135	83,713	113,803	152,208
6%	7,170	16,766	29,607	46,791	69,787	100,562	141,745	196,857
7%	7,383	17,740	32,265	52,638	81,211	121,287	177,495	256,332
8%	7,603	18,774	35,188	59,307	94,744	146,815	223,322	335,737
9%	7,827	19,872	38,403	66,918	110,788	178,290	282,150	441,950
10%	8,059	21,037	41,940	75,602	129,818	217,131	357,752	584,222
11%	8,295	22,273	45,828	85,518	152,398	265,095	454,996	774,992
12%	8,538	23,586	50,103	96,838	179,200	324,351	581,355	1,030,970
13%	8,786	24,976	54,806	112,164	211,020	397,578	741,298	1,374,583
14%	9,043	26,454	59,976	124,521	248,799	488,084	948,807	1,835,890
15%	9,304	28,018	65,660	141,372	293,654	599,948	1,216,015	2,455,144
16%	9,572	29,679	71,910	160,609	346,905	726,194	1,560,032	3,286,173
17%	9,848	31,440	78,778	182,566	410,115	909,004	2,002,792	4,400,869
18%	10,130	33,306	86,326	207,625	485,126	1,119,982	2,572,378	5,895,109
19%	10,419	35,284	94,620	236,216	574,117	1,380,464	3,304,696	7,896,595
20%	10,716	37,380	103,730	268,831	679,652	1,701,909	4,245,610	10,575,154
21%	11,019	39,601	113,736	306,021	804,759	2,098,358	5,435,622	14,156,310
22%	11,330	41,954	124,722	348,416	952,998	2,587,006	7,003,256	18,939,087
23%	11,649	44,446	136,779	396,727	1,128,558	3,188,884	8,989,333	25,319,371
24%	11,976	47,085	150,013	451,758	1,336,360	3,929,683	11,532,334	33,820,458
25%	12,310	49,879	164,530	514,417	1,582,186	4,840,641	14,666,342	45,132,982

<u>CHART 2</u> - Annual Money Chart by Rollie Riesberg, Financial Growth Services

$10,000 Lump Sum at Varying Rates Compounded Annually - End of Year Values

	5th Yr.	10th Yr.	15th Yr.	20th Yr.	25th Yr.	30th Yr.	35th Yr.	40th Yr.
1%	10,510	11,046	11,609	12,201	12,824	13,478	14,166	14,888
2%	11,040	12,189	13,458	14,459	16,406	18,113	19,998	22,080
3%	11,592	13,439	15,579	18,061	20,937	24,272	28,138	32,620
4%	12,166	14,802	18,009	21,911	26,658	32,433	39,460	48,010
5%	12,762	16,288	20,789	26,532	33,863	43,219	55,160	70,399
6%	13,382	17,908	23,965	32,071	42,918	57,434	76,860	102,857
7%	14,025	19,671	27,590	38,696	54,274	76,122	106,765	149,744
8%	14,693	21,589	31,721	46,609	68,484	100,626	147,853	217,245
9%	15,386	23,673	36,424	56,004	86,230	132,676	204,139	314,094
10%	16,105	25,937	41,772	67,274	108,347	174,494	281,024	452,592
11%	16,850	28,394	47,845	80,623	135,854	228,922	385,748	650,008
12%	17,623	31,058	54,735	96,462	170,000	299,599	527,996	930,509
13%	18,424	33,945	62,542	115,230	212,305	391,158	720,685	1,327,815
14%	19,254	37,072	71,379	137,434	264,619	509,501	981,001	1,888,835
15%	20,113	40,455	81,370	163,665	329,189	662,117	1,331,755	2,678,635
16%	21,003	44,114	92,655	194,607	408,742	858,498	1,803,140	3,787,211
17%	21,924	48,068	105,387	231,055	506,578	1,110,646	2,435,034	5,338,687
18%	22,877	52,338	119,737	273,930	626,686	1,433,706	3,279,972	7,503,783
19%	23,863	56,946	135,895	324,294	773,880	1,846,753	4,407,006	10,516,675
20%	24,883	61,917	154,070	373,375	953,962	2,373,763	5,906,682	14,697,715
21%	25,937	67,274	174,494	452,592	1,173,908	3,044,816	7,897,469	20,484,002
22%	27,027	73,046	197,422	533,576	1,442,101	3,897,578	10,534,018	28,470,377
23%	28,153	79,259	223,139	628,206	1,768,592	4,979,128	14,017,769	39,464,304
24%	29,316	85,944	251,956	738,641	2,165,419	6,348,199	18,610,540	54,559,126
25%	30,517	93,132	284,217	867,361	2,646,698	8,077,935	24,651,903	75,231,638

CHART 3 - Lump Sum Money Chart by Rollie Riesberg, Financial Growth Services

THE RULE OF 72

This Rule, based on the Future Value of Money Compounding Rule, tells you How Long it will take for your investment/savings money to <u>double</u> at various rates of return (%).

$$\overline{\smash{\big)}72\ \%}$$

RATE OF RETURN	YEARS TO DOUBLE
72	1
24	3
18	4
12	6
6	12
3	24
1	72

$$18\ \%\ \overline{\smash{\big)}72\ \%}^{\ 4\ \text{Years}} \qquad 6\ \%\ \overline{\smash{\big)}72\ \%}^{\ 12\ \text{Years}}$$

<u>**CHART 4**</u>----Compounding Rule of **72**

FINANCIAL GROWTH SERVICES
'HARD-WORKIN' MONEY HINTS
(What Signs to Watch for – What to Do – When to Do It)

A. **WHEN INTEREST RATES/INFLATION GOES UP!** (Approaching Recession–Bear Market)
1. Stock and bond prices usually go down
2. Real estate prices usually go down
3. Gold and other precious metals prices go up
4. Money market and CD returns go up
5. Consumer goods prices go up

B. **WHEN INTEREST RATES/INFLATION GOES DOWN!** (Economy Growing–Bull Market)
1. Stock and bond prices go up
2. Real estate prices usually go up
3. Gold and other precious metals prices go down
4. Money market and CD returns go down
5. Consumer goods prices go down

C. **ON INTERNATIONAL MONETARY EXCHANGE**
1. Weak Dollar
   a. Helps U.S. exports
   b. Hurts U.S. imports
   c. Hurts exchange rate

2. Strong Dollar
   a. Hurts U.S. exports
   b. Helps U.S. imports
   c. Helps exchange rate

D. **COURSES OF ACTION**
1. If your Debt Interest rate is higher than your savings/Investment Interest Rate-- Pay off your debts.

2. If your Debt Interest rate is lower than your Savings/Investment Interest rate-- put your money into savings/investments.

3. Pay cash for everything-- unless you car borrow at a very low interest rate (much lower than the rate your savings/investments will earn).

4. Mortgage Rates
   a. When Home Mortgage Interest Rates, go up-
      It is a Buyer's Market (Home prices go down)
   b. When Home Mortgage Interests Rates, go down-
      It is a Sellers Market (Home prices go up).

5. To Save and Defer Income Taxes, take advantage of
   a. IRA's: Roth, Traditional, Simple
   b. SEP IRA's and Keogh's
   c. TSA (Tax Sheltered Accounts) 403(b)
   d. Employer sponsored 401k, Thrift/Savings, Profit Sharing, Stock Option and other pension plans.

6. Pay the lowest price for all financial products you are how buying and invest the savings Where the money will work the hardest for you.

NOTE: Financial Products include 1)Home Mortgages 2)Credit cards 3) Home Equity Lines of Credit, etc.

CHART 5 – Hard–Workin' Money Hints

by Rollie Riesberg – Financial Growth Services

Ten rules for money management

1. Plan for the future, major purchases and periodic expenses.

2. Set financial goals. Determine short; mid and long-range financial goals.

3. Know your financial situation. Determine monthly living expenses, periodic expenses and monthly debt payments. Compare outgo to monthly net income. Be aware of your total indebtedness.

4. Develop a realistic budget. Follow your budget as closely as possible. Evaluate your budget. Compare actual expenses with planned expenses.

5. Don't allow expenses to exceed income. Avoid paying only the minimum on your charge cards. Don't charge more every month than you are repaying to your creditors.

6. Save for periodic expenses, such as car and home maintenance. Save five to 10 percent of your net income. Accumulate three to six months' salary in an emergency fund.

7. Pay your own bills on time. Maintain a good credit rating. If you are unable to pay your bills as agreed, contact your creditors and explain your situation. Contact Consumer Credit Counseling Service for professional advice.

8. Distinguish the difference between wants and needs. Take care of your needs first. Money should be spent for wants only after needs have been met.

9. Use credit wisely. Use credit for safety, convenience and planned purchases. Determine the total you can comfortably afford to purchase on credit. Don't allow your credit payments to exceed 20 percent of your net income. Avoid borrowing from one creditor to pay another.

10. Keep a record of daily expenses. Be aware of where your money is going. Use a spending diary to assist you in identifying areas where adjustments need to be made.

CHART 6 – Ten Rules for Money Management

by Rollie Riesberg – Financial Growth Services

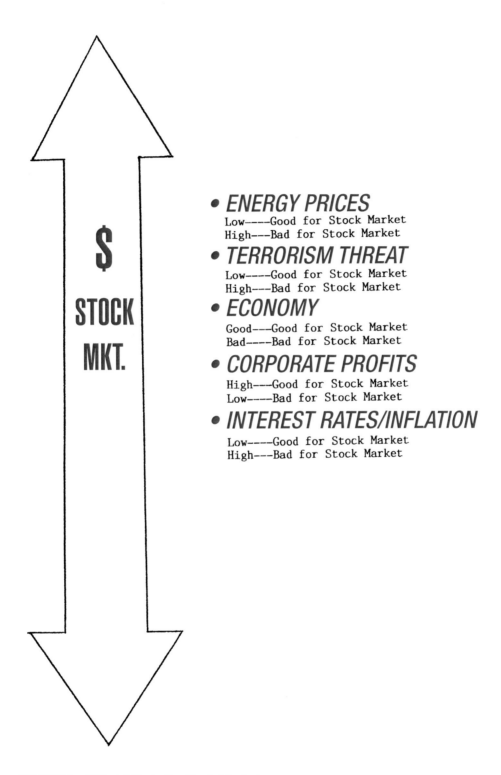

- *ENERGY PRICES*
  Low-----Good for Stock Market
  High----Bad for Stock Market
- *TERRORISM THREAT*
  Low-----Good for Stock Market
  High----Bad for Stock Market
- *ECONOMY*
  Good----Good for Stock Market
  Bad-----Bad for Stock Market
- *CORPORATE PROFITS*
  High----Good for Stock Market
  Low-----Bad for Stock Market
- *INTEREST RATES/INFLATION*
  Low-----Good for Stock Market
  High----Bad for Stock Market

CHART 7 – What Affects the Stock Market

by Rollie Riesberg - Financial Growth Services

TITLE: Why Wealthy People are Wealthy

Question: Why are wealthy people wealthy?

1. Maybe they make big salaries, maybe they don't.

2. They have a lot more money coming in than they have going out.

3. They budget and plan their expenditures wisely.

4. They know how money works hardest. They may even eventually have their money working harder than they are working.

5. They have the right kind and amount of life insurance.

6. They are knowledgeable of tax laws and take full advantage of tax savings techniques available to them.

7. They set financial goals and work toward those goals.

8. They do not procrastinate.

A. How does money work hardest?

1. When it is put into "ownership" investments rather than "loanership" investments - the right place versus the wrong place.

    a. Ownership - Stocks, Mutual Funds, Real Estate, Limited Partnerships, etc.
    b. Loanership - Bonds, Savings Accounts, Treasury Bills/ Bonds, C.D.'s, etc.
    c. Ownership/Loanership Rate of Return/Risk Level:

	Ownership	Loanership
Rate of Return:	loss to no upper limit	low
Risk Level:	low to high	none to low
Stays ahead of Inflation/Taxes:	no to no upper limit	no

2. When you are willing and able to take higher risk.

3. If you are spending your money for the right things.

4. When it is used to buy the right kind and amount of life insurance and amounts of other types of insurance.

5. When income tax savings techniques are fully utilized.

6. When time is on your side.

7. When we give God His share of our income first.

CHART 8 — Wealth   (Page 1 of 2)

B. What is the right kind of life insurance?

1. Term insurance, of course!(in most cases)
Why? Because term insurance is pure protection and nothing else. Other types such as Whole Life are not pure protection; they have a savings feature built into the policy called "cash value" which is surplus premium paid in earlier years of the policy. You do not get this cash value when you die - only the face value or coverage amount of the policy.

2. Do not combine insurance protection and savings - never! You need to save/invest on your own, for yourself - and not for the benefit of the insurance company. Buy only pure protection(term life) and invest the difference - for yourself.

3. Wealthy people have minimal to no life insurance - they are "self insured."

C. How can you save money by knowing about and taking advantage of the tax laws?

1. By sheltering your investment/savings money from income tax until retirement by utilizing the following:

a. IRA
b. Keogh
c. SEP
d. 401K
e. Company Pension/Savings Plan
f. 403B TSA(Tax Sheltered Account)

2. Interest paid on primary and secondary home loans is tax deductible.

3. Business expenses through owning your own business are tax deductible.

CHART 8 – Wealth   (Page 2 of 2)

by Rollie Riesberg - Financial Growth Services

Theme: <u>SHOW HIS LOVE----GIVE</u>

If we died yesterday--God has has already blessed us so much more than we deserve. He has showered us with His love in so many ways. Life itself is one of His many blessings.

We cannot begin to show our appreciation for what He has done for us. In some small way, we can return to Him a portion of what is already His--our money and our service.

The money--we ask ourselves, where is the money going to come from? There is too much month left at the end of the money! Perhaps we are not good enough stewards of the material possessions God has given us, either through our not knowing how to manage our money or through our extravagance, or maybe we are in a lower income situation. Somehow, the money has "slipped through our fingers." How can we be better managers of our money and stop it from slipping through our fingers?

1. By getting what little amount of savings/investment money we have, working harder for us.
2. By taking advantage of all of the tax advantages that are available to us.
3. By having the right kind and amount of insurance protection.
4. By having a properly sized emergency fund set aside so we will not have to rely on credit card "plastic money" purchases to meet emergency needs.
5. By being more selective on what we buy and when we buy (Do we really need it; do we really have to have it now?).
6. By having a budget and staying within those budget limits (Are we living within the boundaries of our income?).
7. By making ourselves set aside a certain amount of money each payday for savings/investment (without fail) just like we do giving God back a portion of the monetary blessings He has made possible for us to have and use (Pay God first, then yourself, then let the bill collectors fight over the rest).

One might think, it is not right to put much emphasis on money and material things. True--money does not buy happiness--but then, neither does poverty. God does not intend for us to be poor. He wants us to use the blessings He has given us (our talents, our intelligence, our knowledge and our time) to His and our best advantage to the glory of His kingdom. We must use our many blessings to help ourselves, our fellowman and to serve God the way He intended.

Think about it--Pray about it-- DO IT!

<u>CHART 9</u> – <u>Giving Back</u>   by Rollie Riesberg – Financial Growth Services

CHAPTER FOURTEEN

OUR TRIBUTE TO LORETTA

LIFE AFTER DEATH

<u>Life</u>: (Psalm 89:47) Remember how short my time is: wherefore hast thou made all men in vain? 48. What man is he that liveth, and shall not see death? Shall he deliver his soul from the hand of the grave? (John 5:24) Verily, verily, I say unto you, He that heareth my word, and believeth on him that sent me, hath everlasting life, and shall not come into condemnation; but is passed from death unto life. 25. Verily, verily, I say unto you, The hour is coming, and now is, when the dead shall hear the voice of the Son of God: and they that hear shall live. 29. And shall come forth; they that have done good, unto the resurrection of life; and they that have done evil, unto the resurrection of damnation.

<u>Death of the Righteous</u>: (II Corinthians 1:9) But we had the sentence of death in ourselves, that we should not trust in ourselves, but in God which raiseth the dead: 10. Who delivered us from so great a death, and doth deliver: in whom we trust that he will yet deliver us.

<u>What Happens Moments After Death</u>?
   The Word of God deals with three great issues everyone must face: life, death and eternity. And there will <u>never</u> be a time when you will not have to face those issues! Consider your eternal destiny. If you're not prepared to die, you're not prepared to live.
   There is '<u>Life After Death</u>'—not extinction or annihilation—
because Jesus teaches it. Your soul will be in existence
somewhere when the sun, moon, and stars have turned to cinders.
   If you have not given your heart to Jesus, moments after you die, you will be in Hell. But to get there, you will have to climb over the Word you've heard, the Holy Spirit's conviction, Mt. Calvary's blood-stained cross, your own conscience, and those who have prayed for you. And once you're there in Hell, you will <u>never</u> come out!
   But you don't have to go to Hell. God loves you, and Jesus died for you! Jesus invites you: "Whosoever will may come." If today you give your heart to Jesus Christ, He will save you and keep you saved for all eternity. Think about it, pray about it—do it!! And please, don't put your <u>destiny</u> at risk!

Rollie's Story

   My precious little angel, Loretta, got cancer and died because of sin in the world. I thank God every day that she is no longer suffering because He rescued her from her cancer.
She is now back home in Heaven, resting in peace, enjoying the <u>ultimate happiness</u> because she is with God, Jesus, her mom, dad, brother and grandparents.

I have learned from going through this experience in my life that love, as created by God, is the <u>best</u> thing in the world, and a broken heart is the worst. As my broken heart is healing, I am growing closer and closer to God and Jesus. I am seeing this as the 'golden opportunity' of my life witnessing, telling others I meet, how very much God and Jesus love us. God loves us so very much, He sent His only begotten Son, Jesus Christ, to die for us and our sins (John 3:16). Please <u>remember</u>, God loves you just the way you are, but He loves you too much to let you stay that way. God does not change us so He can love us, He loves us so He can change us. God is a God of new, fresh beginnings.

My precious Loretta now has a new life in Heaven with eternal life, love, and happiness; and I have a new, happier life here on earth, serving God and Jesus. I thank God for rescuing me from the old me.

It Is OK To Cry

"When you lose a precious loved one,
don't stop yourself from crying,
as long as you remember that God
loves you, and your loved one is now
safe from pain and resting in peace
with God and Jesus in heaven.

Crying cleanses the heart, mind and soul."

· Rollie Riesberg ·

Crying is O.K. because it cleanses the heart, mind and soul. As the author of this Book, I am sharing with you the things you can do to minimize your crying from the loss of a dear loved one:

1) Stay very busy doing the things you love doing and are good at.

2) Concentrate on others who are hurting and in need of help.

3) Every day, pray to God and ask Him to let you know what you can do to help others who are suffering from a broken heart like you have been suffering.

4) Focus on **'Counting Your Blessings'** and not so much on yourself.

5) Think a lot about finding creative ways to be a better witness for God and Jesus.

6) Think more with your heart than with your mind.

7) Place your problems and pain on God's shoulders and He will carry them for you.

8) Pray and talk with God **all of the time** every day, and God will listen and give you guidance and strength as you make your journey through life here on earth. And obey what God tells you to do!

9) Plan for your future in Heaven with God and Jesus and your dear loved ones.

TRIBUTE TO OUR PRECIOUS DECEASED LOVED ONES

Rollie's Tribute to Loretta

Baby Loretta

Delta Air Lines Stewardess

the Day Before
Loretta Went to Heaven

(1) Missing You So...........

My Precious Little Doll:

- I miss your beautiful face and your reassuring smile of
  sunshine and warmth.
- I miss your loving hold-me-tight hugs and your warm
  and tender kisses.
- I miss your heart beating so close and in rhythm with
  mine. You have the biggest, softest heart in the whole
  wide world and in heaven.
 - When we said "I do," I gave you my heart.
 - I miss your caring kindness, sweetness and loving nature.
 - I miss your love here on earth but I know you now love
   me with an even greater love—a heavenly love. You
   were and are so very easy to love. I am falling in love
   with you more and more each and every day.
 - I miss your loving friendship. You were always so easy
    to talk with and understanding.
 - You are my best friend. Now you, God, and Jesus are my
   best friend. I am eternally grateful to you for
   introducing me to God and Jesus! Because of that, I
   will live with you and God and Jesus in Heaven
   forever!
 - I will always love you with all my heart and soul!
   You are My Precious Little Doll!!!

(2) My Letter to Loretta

My Dearest Loretta---

Honey, this world will never be the same because you came. God sent you from Heaven and now He has brought you back home. You saved my life–you brought me to Jesus.

Because of you, _**I Have**_ truly _**Seen The Light**_.

My heart is broken–but I am so happy that you are now at home with God and Jesus and are no longer suffering.

You have been so sweet, kind, loving, caring, and understanding to me, family, friends, and others. You deserve the best God and Heaven has to offer.

I will _**Never Say Goodbye**_ to you–you are my life, hope, happiness and guardian angel. I am eternally grateful to you and God and Jesus!

I love you with all of my heart and soul and I always will! Honey, the best part of me went with you to Heaven–please pray for the other part!

Your loving and devoted husband, always and forever,

Rollie

(2) **My Letter to Loretta**

OUR DECLARATION OF WAR ON SATAN AND SIN—WITH GOD'S AND JESUS'S HELP

There is a constant battle going on between God and Satan (the Devil). God is constantly trying to help us maintain our total faith and trust in Him. The Devil is constantly trying to win us over to him by torturing and tempting us with:
   a) Pain and suffering from the loss of our dear
       loved ones.
   b) Tempting us with <u>big sin</u> things like suicide,
       murder, adultery, crime, etc. which will lead
       us to eternity in hell with the Devil.
   We hereby declare war on the Devil and sin!!!

Rollie's Declaration

Our hearts are broken and shattered because of the pain and suffering and resultant death and loss of our precious loved ones. This was caused by you, Satan, and sin in the world. Your home in Hell is the haven for <u>SIN</u>, and you, the Devil, are the King of Sin! We hereby declare war on <u>you and Sin</u>! You will end up dying a double-death from loneliness, because your supply of nonbelievers who die and go to Hell will dry up, leaving you no new people to influence in living their lives dedicated to sin. We dedicate our lives to serving God and Jesus by showing nonbelievers how very much God and Jesus love them. We will be helping them to convert their lives to Christianity, with them accepting Jesus as their Lord and Savior.   Then they will live happily ever after in heaven when God brings them home.
Satan, may you rot and burn in Hell forever!!!

Loretta and Rollie

"Through The Years"

CHAPTER FIFTEEN

OUR TRIBUTE TO OUR LORD AND SAVIOUR, JESUS CHRIST

We are all so very blessed to have God and Jesus as the foundation and capstone of our lives!

Without God and Jesus, we could not have been able to get through the loss of our dear loved ones.

Through our love, faith, and trust in Jesus, our Lord and Savior and God, our Heavenly Father, we know that our loved ones, who have passed from this earthly home, are resting peacefully and pain-free, for eternity in Heaven.

Thank you God, for giving us that assurance and your love and all of the wonderful things here on earth to enjoy and share with others whom we dearly love. We love You and Your Precious Son more than life itself! Dear Jesus, because of all of the pain and suffering You endured for us on the cross, you have given us the ultimate gift of eternal salvation, eternal love, life, happiness, and peace.

May God's showers of blessings continue to fall upon you and His light of hope continue to shine on you always and forever!!

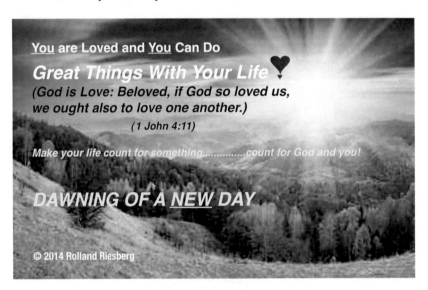

God wants us to use the blessings He has given us (our talents, our intelligence, our knowledge and our time) to His and our best advantage to the glory of His kingdom. We must use our many blessings to help our fellow man, ourselves, and to serve God the way He intended.

God loves you just the way you are, but He loves you too much to let you stay that way. God does not change us so that He can love us, He loves us so that He can change us. God is a God of new, fresh beginnings.

In life, God wants us to work hard, yearn to learn, and in your journey with Him, place your total faith and trust in Him and He will lead you all the way to help you achieve great things for you and for Him. He loves you so much, He sent His Son, Jesus Christ, to die for your sins, that you may have eternal life. Jesus died in your place and your sin debt has been paid in full by His blood on the cross.

Pray to God and thank Him!!!

.......God Bless the Moon and God Blessed Me
By: Loretta C.R. Riesberg

WE ARE 'PEOPLE-PROBLEM' ENGINEERS OF LIFE

   We, the coauthors of these books, are "People-Problem Engineers of Life". We will try to help you fix your 'problems of life' with:
1) Our books written for God and you
2) the use of references from God's Holy Bible and
3) God's love and guidance helping you and us.
However, we cannot fix a broken heart---God fixes broken hearts. And God's precious Son, Jesus, died on the cross to **Save** us from **sin** and eternal **death**. With Jesus in our hearts, minds, and souls, eternal **death** has been replaced with eternal **salvation and life** in Heaven with God, Jesus and our deceased loved ones. And once we die and go to Heaven, God will remove the **sorrow** from us from the loss of our dear loved ones while we were here on earth!

Loretta's & Rollie's Wedding Photo

AUTHOR'S CONTACT INFORMATION

-- LCR ESTATE PLANNING SERVICES, LLC --

www.lcrestateplanningservices.com
R.G. (Rollie) Riesberg
Call: (770) 961-1599
Email: rgriesberg@bellsouth.net
lcr.riesberg@bellsouth.net

-- FINANCIAL GROWTH SERVICES --

www.financialgrowthservices.com
R.G. (Rollie) Riesberg
Call: (770) 961-1599
Email: fingrowserv@bellsouth.net

-- The ROLLAND G. and LORETTA C. RIESBERG FOUNDATION, Inc.—

www.rglcriesbergfoundation.com
Rolland G. (Rollie) Riesberg, President and Chairman
Call: (770) 961-1599
Email: rgriesberg@bellsouth.net
lcr.riesberg@bellsouth.net

THE
ROLLAND G. AND LORETTA C.
RIESBERG FOUNDATION, INC.

Rollie's tribute to God, Jesus and Loretta

Our Photographs Pages

Our Photographs Pages (cont'd)

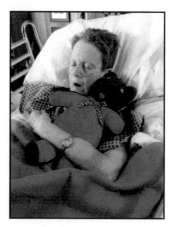

LCR Estate Planning Services, LLC
– Books Division –
www.lcrestateplanningservices.com

Our Books Authors are creative writers of 'Self-Help', 'Problem-Solving', and Christian books. The Authors are becoming widely known as 'People-Problem' Engineers of Life who are here to try to help the readers of their books fix the Problems in their lives.

We are People-Problem Engineers of Life

Growth: There are 4 ways we all Grow in our lives: Physically, Mentally, Spiritually and Financially.

Problems in Our Lives: Once we are grown to adulthood, we may all have many problems in our lives, which can include:
- Marital
- Broken heart from the loss of a dear loved one
- Depression
- Health
- Insecurity
- Financial
- Spiritual

We, the 'People-Problem' Engineers of Life are here to try to help you resolve your problems of life by:

(1) Helping you with your Financial Planning to help you achieve your future financial goals and resolve your existing financial problems.

(2) Helping you and your family resolve Estate Planning problems.

(3) Representing to you, our Books written for you and God, which hold many of the solutions for life's many problems that have occurred in our lives.

We, the Coauthors of our Books, will try to fix your 'problems of life' with:

1) Our books 2) the use of references from God's Holy Bible and 3) God's love and guidance helping you and us.

All of Our MUST READ 'Go To Books' Represented in these Websites:

1. www.godblessthemoongodblessedme.com
2. www.dontsinkswimtosuccess.com
3. www.lifebeforeandafterdeathwithgodslove.com
4. www.howtoavoidthepainandsufferingofprobate.com
5. www.m&pequivalencyamerica.com   (currently in the writing phase)
6. www.gooddadbaddadgoodmombadmom.com   (currently in the writing phase)

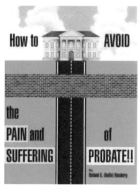

[NOTES:

Things I need to do to AVOID the PAIN and SUFFERING of PROBATE and improve mine and my family's life:

_____

_____

_____

_____

_____

_____

_____

_____

_____

_____

_____

_____